OLD EL PASO®

SUN COUNTRY MEXICAN COOKBOOK

Welcome to new adventures in cooking—Southwestern style.
The recipes in this Old El Paso Cookbook will put you on the trail
to something exciting for a change for meals for your family.
This book was written for you. Why? Because it has:

- Recipes for those not familiar with Mexican flavors—as well
  as new treats for the Mexican food lover
- Easy-to-prepare foods that work into your busy life style
- New ideas that can add excitement to family meals
- Something different for entertaining guests
- Authentic Old Southwestern flavors using today's conveni-
  ence foods and new appliances
- Helpful hints throughout the book to keep you on the trail
  of exciting eating

Welcome to Sun Country where meals are never boring!

Better Homes and Gardens TEST KITCHEN ®

**This seal assures you that every recipe in
Old El Paso Sun Country Mexican Cookbook is tested and approved by the Better Homes and Gardens Test Kitchen.
Each recipe is tested for family appeal,
practicality, and deliciousness.**

Produced by Meredith Publishing Services, 1716 Locust St., Des Moines, Ia., 50336

TABLE OF CONTENTS

WELCOME TO SUN COUNTRY

We wish you could all enjoy El Paso, Texas year 'round. It's a warm, sunshine-drenched place where Spanish, Old West and Mexican cultures blend comfortably. Good food, a leisurely lifestyle and outdoor activities are the things that are really important in this desert setting. This is where Old El Paso Mexican Foods grew up. We began making Mexican food in 1917 and have been satisfying the folks of El Paso (who know these flavors best) for more than 60 years. Now we share these food products across the country. We're delighted that more and more Americans are turning to Mexican foods. Sharing recipes is half the fun. If you can't live in Sun Country, you can still enjoy its flavors.

Only Old El Paso offers you a complete line of Mexican food. In fact, there are 126 Old El Paso products which have been developed to meet your needs.

Pictured below and described here are some of the Old El Paso favorites which you'll identify quickly.

TACO SHELLS, TOSTADA SHELLS AND TACO DINNERS

Old El Paso shells are ground from selected corn, specially seasoned for extra flavor and fried in pure vegetable oil. You'll enjoy interesting variations in their use on page 8 (Meat 'n Potato Tacos) and page 38 (Tuna Tostadas).

TACO SAUCES

Old El Paso sauces are made from fresh vegetables selected in the nearby Mesilla Valley and processed within 24 hours after they are picked. Their seasonings range from mild to hot. Try the Chicken Tacos on page 10.

REFRIED BEANS

Made from selected pinto beans, Old El Paso Refried Beans are lightly flavored with spices, mashed and cooked to a thick consistency. Saucy Beef Tostadas (recipe page 38) is just one of the many tasty ways to use this product.

SEASONING MIX

Old El Paso Taco Seasoning Mix is formulated from quality spices selected and ground to rigid specifications. Be sure to try the Taco-Seasoned Round Steak described on page 68.

TAMALES

These tamales are made from fresh-ground corn, selected cuts of beef and pork, and wrapped the authentically Mexican way.

You'll find a surprising use for tamales on page 64 (Mexican Flank Steak) as well as many other quick-to-fix ideas in this cook book.

GREEN CHILIES

These mild green chilies are grown especially for Old El Paso on nearby farms and picked, roasted and processed in a single day. Try them in Steak and Vegetable Kabobs (page 66) or the appetizer on page 49 (Cheese and Chilies).

ENCHILADA SAUCE

You'll find many uses for this bright, pure flavor, thick sauce (comes both hot and mild). Be sure to try the Cheesy Beef Pie on page 90.

PINTO BEANS AND MEXE-BEANS

These selected whole pinto beans are great products to keep on hand. The Mexe-Beans are combined with a special chili sauce. Try the Bean Soup and Tamale Dumplings on page 36.

Tacos and More Tacos

Meat 'n Potato Tacos

1 pound ground beef
8 ounces (2 cups) frozen hash browns
1/2 medium onion, chopped (1/4 cup)
1 envelope **Old El Paso Taco Seasoning Mix** (1/3 cup)
1 10-ounce can **Old El Paso Tomatoes and Green Chilies**
12 **Old El Paso Taco Shells**
   Lettuce
   Shredded cheddar cheese
   Old El Paso Taco Sauce

In skillet, combine ground beef, hash browns, and onion; cook till meat is brown and onion is tender. Stir in seasoning mix and tomatoes and green chilies; simmer, uncovered, 10 minutes.

Heat taco shells according to package directions. Spoon meat mixture into taco shells; top with lettuce, shredded cheese, and taco sauce. Makes 12 tacos.

Ham and Bean Tacos

8 **Old El Paso Taco Shells**
1 cup diced fully cooked ham
1 tablespoon butter or margarine
1/2 of a 16-ounce can **Old El Paso Refried Beans**
1/4 cup dairy sour cream
1/2 teaspoon chili powder
   Dash garlic powder
   . . . .
1 cup (4 ounces) shredded Monterey Jack cheese
   Shredded lettuce
1 medium tomato, chopped
   Old El Paso Taco Sauce

Warm taco shells according to package directions.

Meanwhile, in small skillet, brown the ham in butter or margarine. Stir in refried beans, sour cream, chili powder, and garlic powder. Cook over low heat, stirring constantly, till heated through. Spoon ham filling into warm taco shells. Sprinkle cheese and lettuce atop each; top with chopped tomato. Pass taco sauce. Makes 8 tacos.

Throw a Taco Party with Ease—All the work for the host and hostess is done before everyone arrives so you can enjoy the function along with the group, too.

The key is to have enough fillings and toppers ready for the taco stuffers.

Plan to use about 1/4 cup meat mixture for each taco. (A pound of cooked meat will give you about 3 cups when chopped. You'll get about 2 cups cooked meat from a pound of ground beef.)

Meat Filling Starters: Prepare an assortment of taco fillings according to the recipe on the back of the **Old El Paso Taco Seasoning Mix** using ground beef, ground lamb, bulk Italian sausage, bulk pork sausage, chopped cooked chicken, chopped cooked ham, or chopped cooked beef.

Taco Toppers: Offer a selection of shredded cheeses, sliced pepperoni, sliced green onion, **Old El Paso Chopped Green Chilies**, chopped **Old El Paso Pickled Chilies Jalapeños**, **Old El Paso Refried Beans** or **Refried Beans with Sausage**, chopped mushrooms, shredded cabbage, shredded carrots, sliced olives, shredded zucchini, radish slices, shredded lettuce, sliced avocado, or cucumber slices.

Taco Sauces: Have on hand a selection of mild to hot sauces such as **Old El Paso's Mild** and **Hot Taco Sauce, Jalapeño Sauce, Picante Sauce, Jalapeño Relish.**

Meat-Filled Tacos

Meat-Filled Tacos

Pictured above

1 pound ground beef or bulk pork
    sausage
1 medium onion, chopped ($\frac{1}{2}$ cup)
1 clove garlic, minced
1 envelope **Old El Paso Taco
    Seasoning Mix** ($\frac{1}{3}$ cup)
$\frac{3}{4}$ cup water

    . . .

12 **Old El Paso Taco Shells**
2 tomatoes, chopped and drained
1 cup (4 ounces) shredded sharp
    cheddar cheese
    Shredded lettuce
    Old El Paso Taco Sauce

In skillet, cook beef or pork, onion, and garlic till meat is brown and onion is tender. Drain off fat. Stir in taco seasoning mix and water. Bring to boiling. Reduce heat and simmer, uncovered, 15 to 20 minutes, stirring occasionally.

    Meanwhile, arrange taco shells on baking sheet lined with paper toweling. Warm in 350° oven for 5 to 10 minutes. Stuff each of the taco shells with some of the meat mixture, tomatoes, cheese, and lettuce; pass taco sauce. Makes 12 tacos.

Cheese Tacos

1 medium onion, chopped (½ cup)
2 tablespoons cooking oil
1 10-ounce can **Old El Paso Tomatoes and Green Chilies**
1 teaspoon dried oregano, crushed

. . .

8 ounces Monterey Jack or longhorn cheese
12 **Old El Paso Taco Shells**
1 avocado, peeled and cut in 12 wedges
1 cup dairy sour cream

Cook onion in hot oil till tender but not brown. Stir in tomatoes and green chilies and oregano. Simmer 20 minutes or till very thick; keep warm.

Cut cheese into 12 strips. Place one strip cheese in each taco shell. Arrange tacos on baking sheet. Bake, uncovered, in 350° oven for 7 to 8 minutes, or till cheese starts to melt. Top cheese with a spoonful of tomato and chilies mixture, an avocado slice, and a dollop of sour cream. Makes 12 tacos.

Chicken Tacos

½ cup chopped onion
2 tablespoons butter or margarine
2 cups diced cooked chicken
1 7½-ounce can **Old El Paso Taco Sauce**
½ teaspoon salt
¼ teaspoon garlic salt

. . .

12 **Old El Paso Taco Shells**
Sliced avocado
Sliced radish
Old El Paso Picante Sauce or **Taco Sauce**

In saucepan, cook onion in butter or margarine till tender but not brown. Stir in chicken, taco sauce, salt, and garlic salt; simmer, uncovered, over low heat for 15 minutes.

Meanwhile, place taco shells on baking sheet. Warm in 350° oven for 5 to 10 minutes. Spoon chicken mixture into taco shells; top with slices of avocado and radish. Pass picante sauce or additional taco sauce, if desired. Makes 12 tacos.

Guacamole

For added interest as a dip, stir in a chopped tomato.

2 large avocados, seeded, peeled and cut up
½ small onion, cut up
½ cup **Old El Paso Tomatoes and Green Chilies** or **Old El Paso Taco Sauce**
1 tablespoon lemon or lime juice
¾ teaspoon salt

In blender container place avocados, onion, tomatoes and green chilies or taco sauce, lemon or lime juice, and salt; cover and blend till smooth. Use as a taco or tostada topping or as a dip with broken taco or tostada shells. Makes about 2 cups.

Consider a Taco Dinner a Staple. Keep a package of **Old El Paso Taco Dinner** on the pantry shelf for a quick and easy dinner. If you don't have ground meat on hand, open up a can of **Old El Paso Refried Beans**, or **Refried Beans with Sausage**, or **Beef Taco Filling** and heat through for a different and tasty filling.

Chop up and pile in any fresh vegetables you happen to have in the refrigerator. Since tacos can be individualized, it's a snap to please anyone at the dinner table.

Green, White, and Red Tacos

Green, White, and Red Tacos

Pictured above in the colors of the Mexican flag

 1 small onion, chopped
 1 tablespoon cooking oil
 1 8-ounce can tomato sauce
 2 **Old El Paso Pickled Chilies Jalapeños,** seeded, rinsed, and chopped
¼ teaspoon salt
 2 cups chopped cooked chicken or pork

    · · ·

12 **Old El Paso Taco Shells**
 2 cups Guacamole (see page 10)
½ cup dairy sour cream

Cook onion in hot oil till tender; stir in tomato sauce, jalapeño peppers, and salt. Simmer, covered, for 5 minutes. Stir in chicken or pork; heat through. Keep warm.

   Meanwhile, place taco shells on baking sheet; heat in 350° oven for 5 to 10 minutes. Spoon a little Guacamole, sour cream, and meat mixture into each taco shell. Makes 12 tacos.

Sun Country Casseroles

Frank-Tamale Pie

Pictured at right

1 cup chopped onion
2 tablespoons butter or margarine
8 ounces frankfurters, cut in
   ½-inch slices
1 15-ounce can **Old El Paso
   Mexe-Beans**
1 12-ounce can whole kernel corn,
   drained
½ to 1 10-ounce can **Old El Paso
   Mild Enchilada Sauce**
1 4-ounce can **Old El Paso Whole
   Green Chilies**, seeded, rinsed,
   and chopped
¼ cup chopped pitted ripe olives
2½ cups cold water
¾ cup yellow cornmeal
½ teaspoon salt
1½ cups (6 ounces) shredded
   American cheese

In large skillet, cook onion in butter or margarine till tender but not brown. Add sliced franks, beans, corn, enchilada sauce (½ to 1 can depending on hotness desired), chilies, and olives. Simmer, uncovered, for 10 minutes, stirring often. Meanwhile, place cold water in medium saucepan; stir in cornmeal and salt. Cook and stir till thickened, about 1 minute after mixture comes to boiling. Add cheese to frank mixture, stirring till melted. Turn frank mixture into 12x7½x2-inch baking dish. Spoon cornmeal batter atop hot mixture, forming a lattice design as shown in picture at right. Bake, uncovered, in 375° oven 25 minutes. Let stand 5 minutes before serving. Makes 6 servings.

Sour Cream-Chili Bake

Pictured on page 7

1 pound ground beef
1 15-ounce can **Old El Paso
   Mexe-Beans**, drained
1 10-ounce can **Old El Paso Hot
   Enchilada Sauce**
1 8-ounce can tomato sauce
1 cup (4 ounces) shredded
   American cheese
1 tablespoon instant minced onion
2 cups coarsely crushed **Old El
   Paso Taco** or **Tostada Shells**
1 cup dairy sour cream
½ cup (2 ounces) shredded
   American cheese

In skillet, brown ground beef; drain off fat. Stir in drained beans, enchilada sauce, tomato sauce, the 1 cup shredded cheese, and the instant minced onion.
   Set aside 1 cup of the crushed taco shells; stir remaining into the meat mixture. Turn into 1½-quart casserole. Bake, covered, in 375° oven for 30 minutes.
   Sprinkle reserved chips around edge of casserole; spoon sour cream atop casserole and sprinkle with remaining cheese. Bake, uncovered, till cheese melts, 2 to 3 minutes. Makes 6 servings.
   Microwave Directions: In 2-quart casserole, crumble ground beef. Add onion; micro-cook on high power, covered, till meat is brown, about 5 minutes, stirring several times to break up meat. Drain off excess fat. Stir in enchilada sauce and tomato sauce. Micro-cook on high power, covered, 5 minutes, stirring once. Stir drained beans, 1 cup of the crushed taco shells, and the 1 cup cheese into meat. Micro-cook, covered, 6 minutes, stirring once. Stir, sprinkle with remaining taco shells, then spread sour cream over top. Sprinkle with remaining cheese. Cook just till sour cream is hot, 30 to 45 seconds. Makes 6 servings.

Frank-Tamale Pie

Beefy Garbanzo Casserole

1 pound ground beef
1 cup chopped onion
2 cloves garlic, minced
. . .
2 15-ounce cans **Old El Paso Garbanzos,** drained
1 15-ounce can tomato sauce
½ cup water
1 teaspoon dried oregano, crushed
½ teaspoon salt
½ teaspoon ground cumin
¼ teaspoon pepper
2 bay leaves

In saucepan, cook ground beef, onion, and garlic till meat is brown and onion is tender. Drain off excess fat. Stir in garbanzo beans, tomato sauce, water, oregano, salt, cumin, pepper, and bay leaves. Heat to boiling. Turn into 1½-quart casserole.

Bake, covered, in 350° oven for 45 minutes. Remove bay leaves; stir to serve. Makes 5 to 6 servings.

Chicken-Cheese Bake

1 10¾-ounce can condensed cream
   of chicken soup
1 8-ounce jar process cheese
   spread
½ cup milk
2 cups diced, cooked chicken
3 tablespoons **Old El Paso Chopped
   Green Chilies**
2 teaspoons instant minced onion
4 cups coarsely crushed **Old El
   Paso Taco** or **Tostada Shells**

In saucepan heat together soup and cheese spread till blended. Gradually stir in milk; add chicken, chilies, and onion. Cook and stir till mixture bubbles. Place *half* the crushed taco shells in 1½-quart casserole. Pour in soup mixture; top with remaining shells. Bake in 350° oven for 20 minutes. Let stand 5 minutes before serving. Makes 4 or 5 servings.

Hot Tamale Bake

1 14½-ounce can **Old El Paso
   Tamales**
2 tablespoons all-purpose flour
1 teaspoon chili powder
¼ teaspoon salt
¼ teaspoon garlic salt
3 beaten eggs
1 16-ounce can cream-style corn
½ cup pitted ripe olives, halved
½ cup (2 ounces) shredded sharp
   cheddar cheese

Drain tamales, reserving sauce. Remove wrappers and slice tamales crosswise; set aside. In mixing bowl, combine reserved tamale sauce, flour, chili powder, salt, and garlic salt. Add eggs, corn, olives, and sliced tamales. Turn into 10x6x2-inch baking dish. Bake, uncovered, in 350° oven for 40 minutes or till set. Sprinkle with cheese. Return to oven to melt cheese, 2 to 3 minutes. Cut in squares to serve. Makes 4 servings.

Hearty Mexican Casserole

The instant coffee crystals give an authentic, yet subtle flavor.

2 pounds ground beef
1 cup chopped onion
2 cloves garlic, minced
2 10-ounce cans **Old El Paso Mild
   Enchilada Sauce**
1 15-ounce can tomato sauce
1 tablespoon instant coffee
   crystals
1½ teaspoons salt
¼ teaspoon pepper
24 **Old El Paso Tortillas** (18 tortillas
   per can)
   Cooking oil
1 8-ounce package cream cheese,
   softened
1 cup water
1½ cups (6 ounces) shredded sharp
   American cheese

In skillet, cook ground beef, onion, and garlic till meat is brown and onion is tender; drain off excess fat. Combine enchilada sauce and tomato sauce. Stir together *2 cups* of the sauce mixture, the instant coffee crystals, salt, pepper, and the meat mixture. Set aside.

Dip tortillas in hot oil till limp, about 5 seconds per side. Drain on paper toweling. Spread one side of each tortilla with softened cream cheese. Place about ¼ cup meat mixture in center of each tortilla; roll up. Place 12 filled tortillas, seam side down, in each of two 12x7½x2-inch baking dishes. Combine the remaining tomato-enchilada sauce mixture and the water. Pour over tortillas. Wrap in foil, label, and freeze one casserole. Bake remaining casserole, covered, in 375° oven for 25 minutes. Uncover; sprinkle with cheese. Return to oven to melt cheese, 2 to 3 minutes. Makes 2 casseroles, 6 servings each.

To bake frozen casserole: Place frozen foil-wrapped casserole in 375° oven; bake 50 minutes. Unwrap; sprinkle with *1½ cups shredded sharp American cheese.* Return to oven to melt cheese, 3 minutes.

Mexican Lasagna

Mexican Lasagna

1 pound ground beef
1/2 cup chopped celery
1/2 cup chopped onion
1 10-ounce can **Old El Paso Tomatoes and Green Chilies**
1 10-ounce can **Old El Paso Mild Enchilada Sauce**
1/4 cup sliced ripe olives
3/4 teaspoon salt
Dash pepper
1/3 cup cooking oil
8 **Old El Paso Tortillas**
1 cup shredded American cheese
1 cup cream-style cottage cheese
1 slightly beaten egg

In skillet, cook ground beef, celery, and onion till meat is brown and vegetables are tender; drain. Stir in tomatoes and green chilies, enchilada sauce, olives, salt, and pepper. Simmer, uncovered, for 10 minutes, stirring occasionally. Heat oil in another skillet. Cut 2 of the tortillas in quarters; cook remaining 6 tortillas and the quarters in hot oil till crisp and brown, about 20 to 30 seconds per side; drain on paper toweling. Set aside quartered tortillas, and break up remaining six. Combine cheeses and egg. Spread one-third of the meat mixture in bottom of 12x7 1/2x2-inch baking dish. Top with half the cheese mixture, then half the broken tortillas. Repeat layers, ending with meat mixture. Top with quartered tortillas. Bake, uncovered, in 350° oven for 30 minutes. Let stand 5 minutes before serving. Makes 4 or 5 servings.

Tostada Casserole

1 pound ground beef
1 15-ounce can tomato sauce
1 envelope **Old El Paso Taco Seasoning Mix** (¹/₃ cup)
2¹/₂ cups coarsely crushed **Old El Paso Taco or Tostada Shells**
1 16-ounce can **Old El Paso Refried Beans**
¹/₂ cup (2 ounces) shredded cheddar cheese

In skillet, brown ground beef; drain off excess fat. Add 1¹/₂ cups of the tomato sauce and the taco seasoning mix, stirring to mix well. Line bottom of 12x7¹/₂x2-inch baking dish with 2 cups of the crushed taco or tostada shells. Spoon meat mixture over shells in baking dish. Combine remaining tomato sauce and the beans; spread over cooked meat mixture.

Bake in 375° oven 25 minutes or till heated through. Sprinkle shredded cheese and remaining crushed shells over the casserole. Return to oven to melt cheese, 2 to 3 minutes more. Makes 6 servings.

Chilies Relleños Bake

1 pound ground beef
¹/₂ cup chopped onion
¹/₂ teaspoon salt
¹/₄ teaspoon pepper

. . .

2 4-ounce cans **Old El Paso Whole Green Chilies,** seeded, rinsed and halved crosswise
1¹/₂ cups (6 ounces) shredded sharp cheddar cheese

. . .

4 beaten eggs
1¹/₂ cups milk
¹/₄ cup all-purpose flour
¹/₂ teaspoon salt
Dash pepper
Old El Paso Taco Sauce

In skillet, cook beef and onion till meat is brown and onion is tender; drain off excess fat. Add the first ¹/₂ teaspoon salt and the ¹/₄ teaspoon pepper. Place half the chilies in 10x6x2-inch baking dish; sprinkle with cheese. Top with meat mixture. Arrange remaining chilies atop. Combine eggs, milk, flour, salt, and the dash pepper; beat till smooth. Pour over chilies. Bake in 350° oven for 45 to 50 minutes or till knife inserted just off center comes out clean. Let stand 5 minutes before serving. Pass taco sauce. Makes 6 servings.

Western Tortilla Casserole

1 pound ground beef
¹/₄ cup chopped onion
1 envelope **Old El Paso Taco Seasoning Mix** (¹/₃ cup)
¹/₄ teaspoon salt
1 cup water
¹/₄ cup **Old El Paso Taco Sauce**
1 10-ounce package frozen chopped spinach
³/₄ cup diced cooked ham
Cooking oil
12 **Old El Paso Tortillas**
1 cup dairy sour cream
1 cup (4 ounces) shredded Monterey Jack cheese

In skillet, cook beef and onion till meat is brown and onion is tender. Drain off excess fat. Stir in dry taco seasoning mix, salt, water, and taco sauce. Add frozen spinach and ham. Cover and simmer till spinach thaws, breaking up spinach block with fork. Simmer, covered, 5 minutes. In small skillet, heat oil. Dip tortillas, one at a time, into oil just till soft and limp, about 5 to 10 seconds. Drain on paper toweling.

To assemble casserole, spoon ¹/₃ cup meat mixture onto each tortilla. Roll up; place, seam side down, in greased 13x9x2-inch baking dish. Cover and bake in 350° oven for 30 to 35 minutes. Uncover; spread sour cream over tortillas. Sprinkle cheese over all. Return to oven to heat sour cream and melt cheese, about 5 minutes. Makes 6 servings.

Easy-Does-It Casserole

2 pounds ground beef
2 medium onions, chopped
1/2 teaspoon salt
1/2 teaspoon garlic salt
1/2 teaspoon ground cumin
1/4 teaspoon pepper
2 10-ounce cans **Old El Paso Mild Enchilada Sauce**
12 **Old El Paso Tostada Shells or Tortillas**
2 cups (8 ounces) shredded cheddar cheese

In skillet, cook ground meat and onions till meat is brown and onion is tender. Drain off excess fat. Stir in salt, garlic salt, cumin, and pepper. Stir in enchilada sauce. In 13x9x2-inch baking dish, layer *half* the tostada shells, meat sauce, and cheese; repeat tostada and meat layers. Cover and bake in 350° oven for 30 minutes. Uncover and sprinkle with remaining cheese. Bake 10 minutes more. Makes 8 servings.

Enchilada-Style Casserole

1 pound beef stew meat, cut in 1/2-inch cubes
1 10 1/4-ounce can beef gravy
1 10-ounce can **Old El Paso Mild Enchilada Sauce**
1 4-ounce can **Old El Paso Whole Green Chilies**, seeded, rinsed, and chopped
1/4 cup chopped onion
1/2 cup water
1/2 teaspoon salt
6 **Old El Paso Tortillas**
Cooking oil
2 tablespoons cornstarch
2 tablespoons cold water
1 cup (4 ounces) shredded cheddar cheese

In large saucepan, combine meat, gravy, enchilada sauce, chilies, onion, the 1/2 cup water, and the salt; heat to boiling. Reduce heat; simmer, covered, for 1 hour or till meat is tender. Remove from heat.

Dip tortillas in hot oil till limp, about 5 seconds per side. Drain on paper toweling. Using slotted spoon, lift meat from sauce; divide among tortillas. Roll up tortillas; place seam side down in greased 12x7 1/2x2-inch baking dish. Blend together cornstarch and the cold water; stir into sauce. Cook and stir till bubbly; pour over tortillas. Bake, uncovered, in 350° oven for 20 minutes. Sprinkle with cheese. Return to oven to melt cheese, 2 to 3 minutes. Makes 6 servings.

Bean and Potato Taco Pie

1/4 cup butter or margarine
1/2 cup milk
1 envelope **Old El Paso Taco Seasoning Mix** (1/3 cup)
2 cups instant mashed potato flakes
. . .
1 pound ground beef
1/2 cup chopped onion
1 16-ounce can **Old El Paso Refried Beans**
1/2 cup bottled barbecue sauce
1/4 cup water
. . .
1 cup (4 ounces) shredded cheddar cheese
1 cup shredded lettuce
1 medium tomato, chopped

In saucepan, melt butter or margarine. Add milk and *2 tablespoons* of the dry taco seasoning mix. Remove from heat and stir in potato flakes. Press mixture over bottom and up sides of ungreased 10-inch pie plate.

In skillet, cook ground beef and onion till meat is brown and onion is tender. Drain off excess fat. Stir in beans, barbecue sauce, water, and the remaining taco seasoning mix. Cook and stir till bubbly. Turn into prepared crust. Bake, uncovered, in 350° oven for 30 to 35 minutes. Top with cheese, lettuce, and tomato. Makes 6 servings.

Quick-Draw Dishes

Mexi-Chicken Skillet

2 cups cubed cooked chicken
1 11-ounce can condensed cheddar cheese soup
1 8-ounce can tomatoes, cut up
½ cup uncooked packaged precooked rice
2 tablespoons **Old El Paso Chopped Green Chilies**
1 15-ounce can **Old El Paso Bean Tamales**

In skillet, combine the cooked chicken, cheese soup, tomatoes, rice, and green chilies. Drain sauce from tamales and add to chicken mixture. Cover and simmer 5 minutes over low heat. Meanwhile, remove wrappers from tamales; cut tamales into 1-inch pieces. Place pieces atop chicken mixture. Cover; cook over low heat till tamales are heated through, about 10 minutes. Makes 4 servings.

Old El Paso Chili Con Carne

1 pound ground beef
½ cup chopped onion
¼ cup chopped green bell pepper
1 clove garlic, minced
1 envelope **Old El Paso Chili Seasoning Mix** (⅓ cup)
1 16-ounce can tomatoes, cut up
⅔ cup water
1 4-ounce can **Old El Paso Whole Green Chilies**, seeded, rinsed, and chopped
Hot cooked rice

In skillet, combine ground beef, onion, green pepper, and garlic. Cook till meat is brown and vegetables are tender. Stir in chili seasoning mix, tomatoes, water, and chilies. Cover and simmer 20 minutes, stirring occasionally. Serve atop hot cooked rice. Makes 4 servings.

Microwave Cooking Directions: In 2-quart casserole, crumble ground beef. Add onion, green pepper, and garlic. Micro-cook, covered, on high power, till meat is browned, about 5 minutes, stirring 2 or 3 times to break up meat. Drain off fat.

Stir in tomatoes, water, green chilies, and chili seasoning mix. Micro-cook, covered, 10 minutes, stirring 3 times. Serve over hot cooked rice.

Southwestern Pizzas

1 13¾-ounce package hot roll mix
1 cup warm water (110°)
. . .
1 10-ounce can **Old El Paso Mild Enchilada Sauce**
2 tablespoons **Old El Paso Chopped Green Chilies**
2 tablespoons chopped onion
4 ounces bulk pork sausage, cooked and drained
4 ounces sliced pepperoni
1 2-ounce can anchovy fillets, drained (optional)
1 cup (4 ounces) shredded Mozzarella cheese
½ cup grated Parmesan cheese
½ medium green pepper, sliced
1 3-ounce can sliced mushrooms, drained
¼ cup sliced pitted ripe olives
Snipped parsley

Prepare hot roll mix according to package directions except use warm water and omit the egg. Do not let rise. Cut dough into four portions. With oiled hands, shape dough into any desired shape on two baking sheets. Crimp edges of dough to make a raised edge. Bake in 450° oven for 6 minutes. Combine enchilada sauce, green chilies, and chopped onion. Spread about ⅓ cup sauce mixture on each pizza. Top with meats, cheeses, and vegetables. Sprinkle with snipped parsely, if desired. Return pizzas to oven. Bake in 450° oven till cheese is melted and edges of dough are browned, about 8 minutes more. Makes 4 individual pizzas.

Mexicali Casserole

Mexicali Casserole

Pictured above

1 14½-ounce can **Old El Paso Tamales**

1 20-ounce can yellow hominy, drained

1 4-or 5-ounce can Vienna sausages, cut in thirds

1 10½-ounce can condensed cream of chicken soup

1 14½-ounce can **Old El Paso Tamales**

¼ cup (1 ounce) shredded sharp cheddar cheese

Remove wrappers from the first can tamales; cut tamales in thirds. Combine the cut tamales, the hominy, sausages, and soup; turn into 1½-quart casserole. Bake, uncovered, in 350° oven for 35 to 40 minutes. Remove wrappers from second can of tamales; cut tamales diagonally in half. Garnish top of casserole with cut tamales. Sprinkle cheese atop. Return to oven to melt cheese and heat top tamales. Makes 6 servings.

Pecos Ham

For a zestier dish, stir in a little **Old El Paso Jalapeño Relish.**

3 cups chopped fully cooked ham
2 cups (8 ounces) shredded
    Monterey Jack cheese
1 8-ounce can tomato sauce
1 4-ounce can **Old El Paso Whole
    Green Chilies,** seeded, rinsed,
    and chopped
½ cup finely chopped onion
    · · ·
    Mexican Muffins (recipe below)

Crockery Cooker Directions: In crockery cooker combine the chopped ham, cheese, tomato sauce, green chilies, and onion. Cover; cook on low-heat setting for 2 hours. To serve split **Mexican Muffins.** Spoon ham mixture over muffins. Makes 6 servings.

Mexican Muffins

For one batch of zingy muffins substitute **Old El Paso Pickled Chilies Jalapeños** for the Green Chilies.

2 cups all-purpose flour
2 tablespoons sugar
1 tablespoon baking powder
⅛ teaspoon chili powder
1 beaten egg
1 8-ounce can cream-style corn
⅓ cup milk
3 tablespoons cooking oil
2 tablespoons **Old El Paso Chopped
    Green Chilies**
2 tablespoons chopped canned
    pimiento

Stir together flour, sugar, baking powder, and chili powder. Combine egg, cream-style corn, milk, oil, chilies, and pimiento; add to dry ingredients, stirring just till moistened. Fill greased muffin pans ⅔ full. Bake in 400° oven for 20 to 25 minutes. Makes 12.

Old El Paso to the Rescue—Some **Old El Paso** convenience items on the pantry shelf can be mighty handy when you're not in the mood for cooking or when you return home and find the refrigerator bare.

• Keep **Old El Paso Beef Taco Filler** or a can of **Old El Paso Refried Beans with Sausage** on hand to team with an **Old El Paso Taco Dinner.**

• A quick lunch of **Old El Paso Chili with Beans** or **Chili Con Carne** and a sandwich can save the day.

• Canned **Old El Paso Beef Enchiladas** or **Beef Tamales** quickly pick you up after any winter outdoor activity.

• Stash **Old El Paso Mexi Pickles** or **Hot Pickled Yellow Chilies** on the shelf for a perky garnish on company dinners. They're a great low-cal nibble, too.

Camper's Mexican Hash

For hearty eating in the great out-of-doors

2 15-ounce cans roast beef hash
1 16-ounce can tomatoes, drained
   and cut up
1 4-ounce can **Old El Paso Whole
   Green Chilies,** seeded, rinsed,
   and chopped
   . . .
1 cup (4 ounces) shredded
   Monterey Jack cheese

In a skillet, stir together hash, tomatoes, and chilies. Bring to boiling. Reduce heat; simmer, stirring often, 15 to 20 minutes or till excess liquid evaporates. Sprinkle cheese atop hash mixture. Cover and heat till cheese melts, about 2 minutes. Makes 4 servings.

Rio Grande Meat Loaf

Perfect for a buffet—every serving is individual. They can be made ahead and their smaller size takes less time to bake.

2 pounds ground beef
1 15-ounce can **Old El Paso Spanish
   Rice**
2 eggs
1/4 cup instant minced onion
1/2 teaspoon salt

Combine ground beef, Spanish rice, eggs, onion, and salt. Shape into 8 or 10 individual loaves or put in 10 custard cups. Bake in 350° oven for 35 minutes. Makes 8 to 10 servings.

Vegetable-Tortilla Rolls

Next time try this filling atop **Old El Paso Tostada Shells** for a stack-up bonanza.

8 **Old El Paso Tortillas**

1 1/2 cups (6 ounces) shredded Swiss
   cheese
1 1/2 cups shredded lettuce
1 small cucumber, chopped
1 3-ounce can chopped mushrooms,
   drained
1 cup Guacamole (recipe on page 10)
   Old El Paso Taco Sauce

Wrap tortillas tightly in foil. Heat in 350° oven about 10 minutes or till warm. Divide Swiss cheese, lettuce, cucumber, and mushrooms among the tortillas. Spoon Guacamole atop; sprinkle with taco sauce. Roll up filled tortillas. Makes 8 rolls.

Chili-Cheese Franks

2 15-ounce cans **Old El Paso Chili
   With Beans**
1 11-ounce can condensed cheddar
   cheese soup
2 tablespoons instant minced
   onion
1 pound frankfurters (8 to 10
   franks)
   . . .
8 to 10 frankfurter buns, split and
   toasted
   Coarsely crushed **Old El Paso
   Taco or Tostada Shells**

In large saucepan, combine chili with beans, soup, and onion. Add frankfurters; heat to boiling. Simmer mixture 5 minutes to blend flavors. Place frankfurter on bun; top with chili-cheese sauce and sprinkle with crushed taco shells. Makes 8 to 10 servings.

Skillet Suppers

Hearty Fiesta Burgers

Pictured at right

- 1 slightly beaten egg
- ¾ cup fine saltine cracker crumbs (21 crackers)
- ¼ cup **Old El Paso Taco Sauce**
- 2 teaspoons instant minced onion
- ¼ teaspoon salt
- 1 pound ground beef

. . .

- 1 10½-ounce can condensed cream of mushroom soup
- 1 15-ounce can **Old El Paso Mexe-Beans**, drained
- 1 4-ounce can **Old El Paso Whole Green Chilies**, seeded, rinsed, and chopped
- ½ cup (2 ounces) shredded cheddar cheese

In mixing bowl, combine egg, cracker crumbs, taco sauce, onion, and salt; add ground beef and mix well. Shape into 6 patties, about 3 inches in diameter. In 12-inch skillet, brown patties on both sides. Pour soup over meat; top with beans and green chilies. Cook, covered, over low heat 10 minutes. Sprinkle with cheese; cover and heat till cheese melts, about 2 minutes. Makes 6 servings.

Mexican-Style Steak

- 1½ pounds beef round steak, cut in serving-size pieces
- ⅛ teaspoon garlic powder
- 2 tablespoons cooking oil
- 1 15-ounce can **Old El Paso Chili Bean Tamales**
- 1 10-ounce can **Old El Paso Mild Enchilada Sauce**
- ¼ cup water

Pound the round steak on both sides; sprinkle with garlic powder. In skillet, brown the steak in hot oil. Drain off excess fat. Drain tamales, reserving sauce. Remove wrappers from tamales, and cut tamales in thirds; set aside. Stir together the reserved tamale sauce, enchilada sauce, and water. Pour over steak in skillet. Cover and simmer over low heat till meat is tender, about 45 minutes. Add tamale pieces and cook 10 minutes more. Makes 6 servings.

Tex-Mex Skillet

- 1 envelope all-purpose meat marinade
- 1 16-ounce can tomatoes, cut up
- 1½ pounds beef round steak, cut in thin strips
- 1 4-ounce can **Old El Paso Whole Green Chilies**, seeded, rinsed, and chopped
- 1 teaspoon sugar
- 1 teaspoon ground cumin
- 1 clove garlic, minced
- 1 16-ounce can **Old El Paso Refried Beans**
- 2 cups cooked rice
- ½ cup dairy sour cream
- ½ cup (2 ounces) shredded cheddar cheese
  Coarsely crushed **Old El Paso Taco or Tostada Shells**

In 12-inch skillet, combine dry meat marinade and undrained tomatoes. Stir in steak strips. Let stand 10 minutes. Stir in chilies, sugar, cumin, and garlic. Bring to boiling; reduce heat and simmer, uncovered, 15 minutes, stirring occasionally. Stir in beans and rice; heat through. Top with sour cream and a ring of cheddar cheese. Cover and heat to melt the cheese, about 2 minutes. Serve over crushed taco or tostada shells. Makes 6 to 8 servings.

Southwestern Swiss Steak
Pictured at right

½ to ¾-pound boneless beef round
   steak, cut ¾-inch thick
2 tablespoons all-purpose flour
½ teaspoon salt
   · · ·
1 10-ounce can **Old El Paso
   Tomatoes and Green Chilies**
¼ cup chopped celery
¼ cup chopped carrot
1 tablespoon chopped onion
   · · ·
2 tablespoons shredded American
   or Monterey Jack cheese

Cut meat into 2 portions. Mix flour and salt; pound into meat. Set aside remaining flour. Brown meat in small amount of hot oil, about 1 tablespoon. Place meat in shallow baking dish. Blend reserved flour mixture into drippings in skillet. Add tomatoes and green chilies, celery, carrot, and onion. Cook, stirring constantly, till mixture boils. Pour over meat. Cover and bake in 350° oven for 1 hour or till meat is tender. Sprinkle cheese over meat. Makes 2 servings.

Camp-Out Burritos

12 **Old El Paso Tortillas**
1 16-ounce can **Old El Paso Refried
   Beans**
   Salt
   Pepper
   Chili powder
1 8-ounce block sharp cheddar or
   Monterey Jack cheese
1 4-ounce can **Old El Paso Whole
   Green Chilies,** seeded and rinsed
¼ cup cooking oil

Spread each tortilla with 2 to 3 tablespoons refried beans; sprinkle each with a little salt, pepper, and chili powder. Cut cheese into 12 julienne strips or sticks, 4 to 5 inches long. Place one cheese stick atop bean mixture on each tortilla. Slice chilies lengthwise into 12 strips; place atop cheese. Roll up tortillas. In 10-inch skillet, heat oil over open fire. Cook half the burritos at a time over medium heat, till tortillas are crisp and cheese just begins to melt, 4 to 6 minutes, turning occasionally. Makes 4 to 6 servings.

Olé Skillet Supper

6 **Old El Paso Tortillas**
2 tablespoons butter or margarine
6 eggs
¼ teaspoon garlic salt
1 tablespoon butter or margarine
   · · ·
1 10-ounce can **Old El Paso Mild
   Enchilada Sauce**
¼ cup sliced ripe olives
2 tablespoons sliced green onion
   · · ·
½ cup (2 ounces) shredded
   Monterey Jack cheese
½ cup dairy sour cream

Tear or cut tortillas into 1-inch pieces. In skillet, cook tortillas in the 2 tablespoons butter or margarine, stirring to coat well. Cook till slightly crisp, about 5 minutes. Remove from skillet; set aside. Beat eggs and garlic salt. Add remaining butter to same skillet; pour in eggs. Continue cooking and stirring till eggs are the consistency of scrambled eggs. Combine enchilada sauce, olives, and onion; stir into eggs with tortillas. Sprinkle with cheese. Cover and cook over low heat till heated through, 5 to 8 minutes. Dollop sour cream atop. Cover and cook 1 minute more. Makes 4 servings.

Southwestern Foods Kids Can Fix

Easy Enchiladas

1 cup (8 ounces) cream-style cottage cheese
1/2 cup dairy sour cream
1/4 teaspoon salt
Dash pepper
6 **Old El Paso Tortillas**
Cooking oil
6 slices bologna
1/2 of 4-ounce can **Old El Paso Whole Green Chilies**, seeded, rinsed, and cut in 6 strips
1 10-ounce can **Old El Paso Mild Enchilada Sauce**

Combine cottage cheese, sour cream, salt, and pepper. Reserve 1/4 cup of the mixture and set aside. Cook tortillas in hot oil for 10 seconds till limp. Drain on paper toweling. Cover each tortilla with 1 slice bologna. Spoon about 1 heaping tablespoon of the cottage cheese mixture atop. Top with a strip of green chili; roll up. Place, seam side down in 10x6x2-inch baking dish. Combine reserved cottage cheese mixture and enchilada sauce; pour over tortillas. Bake, covered, in 350° oven for 40 to 45 minutes till heated through. Makes 6 servings.

Quick Frank Kabobs

Pictured on page 6

2 4-ounce cans **Old El Paso Whole Green Chilies**, seeded and rinsed
8 frankfurters, cut crosswise in thirds
1 16-ounce can whole new potatoes, drained
1/4 cup horseradish mustard
1/4 cup catsup
1/4 cup **Old El Paso Taco Sauce**
2 tablespoons cooking oil

Slit chilies lengthwise in fourths. Wrap one strip of chili around each piece of frankfurter. Thread onto skewers along with potatoes. Combine mustard, catsup, taco sauce, and oil. Grill kabobs over medium coals for 10 minutes, turning often and brushing frequently with mustard mixture. (Or, broil 4 inches from heat for 6 to 8 minutes, turning and brushing with sauce often.) Makes 4 to 6 servings.

Chili-Cheeseburgers

8 hamburger buns, split and toasted
2 15-ounce cans **Old El Paso Chili Con Carne, No Beans**
1/2 cup sour cream dip with French onion

. . .

8 slices (8 ounces) American cheese

Spread bottom of each toasted hamburger bun with 1/4 cup chili without beans. Top with 1 tablespoon French onion sour cream dip. Broil till heated through, 4 to 5 minutes. Top each sandwich with one cheese slice and broil till cheese melts, 1 minute more. Makes 8 sandwiches.

Tamale-Frank Bake

1 15-ounce can **Old El Paso Chili Beans Tamales**
16 ounces frankfurters, cut up
1 11½-ounce can condensed chili beef soup
1 8-ounce can tomato sauce
½ cup (2 ounces) shredded cheddar cheese

. . .

1 cup crushed **Old El Paso Taco** or **Tostada Shells**

Drain tamales, reserving sauce. Remove wrappers from tamales and cut each tamale in thirds.

In 1½-quart casserole, combine the reserved tamale sauce, frankfurters, soup, and tomato sauce. Top with tamales. Cover and bake in 350° oven for 35 minutes. Top with cheese and bake, uncovered, 10 minutes more. Serve topped with crushed taco or tostada shells. Makes 6 servings.

Tamale Casserole

1 package spaghetti dinner with meat sauce and cheese

. . .

1 14½-ounce can **Old El Paso Tamales**
1 16-ounce can whole kernel corn, drained
2 teaspoons chili powder

Break spaghetti from dinner mix into pieces; cook according to package directions, omitting salt. Drain.

Remove wrappers from tamales. Halve 3 tamales and set aside. Cut up remaining tamales and stir into spaghetti along with meat sauce from mix, the corn, and chili powder. Spoon into 1½-quart casserole, top with reserved tamales and cheese from mix. Bake in 350° oven for 45 minutes. Makes 6 servings.

Frankly Easy Meals for Kids. Start with a hot dog and the meal is almost ready to serve. Try one of these ideas:
• Start with sliced frankfurters instead of ground beef for Tacos or Tostadas.
• Spread a warm tortilla with **Old El Paso Chili Con Carne** and wrap it around a frank. Wrap in foil and heat in the oven or wrap with paper or clear plastic wrap and heat in the microwave.

• Dress up the top of a hot dog in a bun with heated **Old El Paso Chili Con Carne** and shredded cheddar cheese.
• Slice franks into a steaming pot of **Old El Paso Chili Con Carne.** Served topped with crushed Taco or Tostada Shells and a sprinkling of shredded Monterey Jack.
• Cut franks into quarters, combine with a can of **Old El Paso Spanish Rice,** and heat. Serve with a salad for a speedy lunch.

Budget-Corralling Meals

Mexican Deviled Eggs

Pictured at right

  3 hard-cooked eggs
  2 tablespoons mayonnaise or salad
     dressing
 1/2 teaspoon vinegar
 1/2 teaspoon prepared mustard
     Dash salt
     Dash pepper

. . .

  2 tablespoons chopped onion
  1 tablespoon butter or margarine
  2 teaspoons all-purpose flour
  1 10-ounce can **Old El Paso
     Tomatoes and Green Chilies**
  2 tablespoons fine dry bread
     crumbs
  2 teaspoons butter or margarine,
     melted

Prepare *Deviled Eggs:* Halve hard-cooked eggs lengthwise; remove yolks and mash. Blend in mayonnaise, vinegar, mustard, salt, and pepper. Refill whites; set aside.

In small saucepan, cook onion in the 1 tablespoon butter till tender; blend in flour. Add tomatoes and green chilies, a dash salt, and a dash pepper. Cook and stir till mixture thickens and bubbles. Pour mixture into 2 individual casseroles. Arrange 3 Deviled Egg halves in each. Combine crumbs and the melted butter; sprinkle over eggs. Bake in 425° oven for 10 minutes. Makes 2 servings.

Chili Manicotti

  2 tablespoons chopped onion
  1 small clove garlic, minced
  1 tablespoon cooking oil
  1 15-ounce can **Old El Paso Chili
     with Beans**
  3 or 4 manicotti shells

. . .

  1 beaten egg
 3/4 cup cream-style cottage cheese,
     drained
 1/2 cup (2 ounces) shredded
     American cheese
  2 tablespoons **Old El Paso Chopped
     Green Chilies**

Cook onion and garlic in hot oil till tender; stir in chili. Cook manicotti in boiling salted water till tender, 15 to 20 minutes. Drain. Cut shells in half crosswise, if necessary to fit two individual baking dishes or a 6½x6½x2-inch baking dish.

Combine egg, cottage cheese, *half* the American cheese, and the chilies. Spoon cheese mixture into manicotti. Pour *half* the chili mixture into the two individual baking dishes or the 6½x6½x2-inch baking dish. Top with stuffed manicotti. Pour remaining chili mixture over, being sure manicotti are coated. Bake, covered, in 350° oven for 35 to 40 minutes. Uncover; sprinkle with remaining cheese. Return to oven to melt cheese, 2 to 3 minutes. Let stand 5 minutes before serving. Makes 2 servings.

Chilies Relleños Casserole

  6 beaten eggs
  3 cups (24 ounces) cream-style
     cottage cheese
 3/4 cup finely crushed rich round
     crackers (18 crackers)
  1 4-ounce can **Old El Paso Whole
     Green Chilies,** seeded, rinsed,
     and chopped
 3/4 cup (3 ounces) shredded cheddar
     cheese
 3/4 cup (3 ounces) shredded
     Monterey Jack cheese

Combine eggs, cottage cheese, cracker crumbs, chilies, and half the shredded cheddar and Monterey Jack cheeses. Turn into a 10x6x2-inch baking dish. Bake in 350° oven for 45 minutes or till knife inserted just off center comes out clean. Sprinkle with remaining cheeses; return to oven to melt cheese, 2 to 3 minutes. Let stand 5 minutes before serving. Makes 6 servings.

Stuffed Tomato Cups

Pictured at right

4 large tomatoes
  Salt
  Dried basil leaves, crushed
½ pound ground beef
¼ cup chopped onion
¼ cup **Old El Paso Chopped Green Chilies**
½ envelope (about 2 tablespoons) **Old El Paso Enchilada Sauce Mix**
½ cup herb-seasoned stuffing croutons
4 teaspoons grated parmesan cheese

Cut tops off tomatoes; scoop out pulp. Chop tops and pulp; drain. Cut sawtooth edges around shells; invert shells to drain. Sprinkle inside with a little salt and basil. In skillet, brown beef with onion; drain off fat. Stir in tomato pulp, chilies, seasoning mix, and croutons; stuff shells. Sprinkle tomatoes with cheese. Place in shallow baking dish; fill dish with ½-inch water. Bake in 375° oven for 25 to 30 minutes. Trim with parsley, if desired. Makes 4 servings.

Mexican Meatball Bake

Enough freeze-ahead meatballs for three casseroles.

3 beaten eggs
¾ cup milk
3 cups soft bread crumbs (about 4½ slices)
½ cup finely chopped onion
2 teaspoons salt
3 pounds ground beef

• • •

1 5-ounce jar cheese spread
¼ cup milk
1 10-ounce can **Old El Paso Mild Enchilada Sauce**
1 20-ounce can yellow hominy, drained
2 tablespoons **Old El Paso Chopped Green Chilies**
2 cups coarsely crushed **Old El Paso Taco or Tostada Shells**

To prepare meatballs: In large mixing bowl, combine beaten eggs, the ¾ cup milk, the bread crumbs, chopped onion, and salt; add meat and mix well. Shape meat mixture into 6 dozen 1-inch balls. Place half the meatballs in 15x10x1-inch baking pan. Bake in 375° oven for 25 to 30 minutes. Remove from pan and cool; repeat with remaining meatballs.

Place cooled meatballs on baking sheet; freeze firm. Using 24 meatballs per package, wrap meatballs in moisture-vaporproof material. Seal, label, and freeze. Makes 6 dozen.

For casserole: In oven-going skillet, blend cheese spread with the remaining ¼ cup milk over low heat; stir in enchilada sauce. Add 24 frozen meatballs, hominy, and chilies. Bring to boiling; stir occasionally. Sprinkle with crushed taco shells. Bake in 350° oven for 30 to 35 minutes. Makes 4 to 6 servings.

Monterey Fondue Bake

6 slices firm-textured white bread
  Butter or margarine
4 beaten eggs
2½ cups milk
1 teaspoon salt
1½ cups (6 ounces) shredded Monterey Jack cheese
1 12-ounce can Mexican-style corn
1 4-ounce can **Old El Paso Whole Green Chilies**, seeded, rinsed, and drained
  Old El Paso Taco Sauce

Spread bread slices lightly with butter or margarine. Cut bread in ½-inch cubes; set aside. In large bowl combine eggs, milk, and salt; stir in bread cubes, cheese, corn, and chilies. Turn into 8x8x2-inch baking dish. Let stand 1 hour at room temperature. Bake in 350° oven for 55 to 60 minutes or till knife inserted just off-center comes out clean. Serve with taco sauce, if desired. Makes 6 servings.

Caballero Sandwiches

Tamale Hero Sandwiches

3 hero buns
1/4 cup **Old El Paso Chopped Green Chilies**
1 tablespoon instant minced onion
1 15-ounce can **Old El Paso Chili with Beans**
1 14 1/2-ounce can **Old El Paso Tamales**
3/4 cup (3 ounces) shredded sharp cheddar cheese

Slice hero buns in half lengthwise and toast. Stir green chilies and onion into chili; spread buns with chili mixture. Remove wrappers; split tamales lengthwise and arrange atop chili. Sprinkle with shredded cheese. Place under broiler for 10 minutes or till cheese melts and sandwiches are heated through. Makes 6 open-faced sandwiches.

Billy-The-Kid Sandwiches

3 cups chopped cooked beef
1 16-ounce can **Old El Paso Refried Beans**
1 7 1/2-ounce can **Old El Paso Taco Sauce**
1/3 cup sliced pitted ripe olives
1 envelope **Old El Paso Chili Seasoning Mix** (1/3 cup)
24 **Old El Paso Taco Shells**, heated **or** hamburger buns, split and toasted
1/2 medium head lettuce, shredded
2 tomatoes, chopped
1 cup (4 ounces) shredded sharp American cheese
  Old El Paso Picante or Hot Taco Sauce

In large skillet or saucepan, combine beef, refried beans, taco sauce, olives, and chili seasoning mix. Cover and simmer till mixture is heated through, about 20 minutes; stir often. Spoon about 1/4 cup mixture into each heated taco shell or hamburger bun; top with a little lettuce, tomato, and cheese. Pass picante sauce. Makes 2 dozen.

Crockery Cooker Directions: In electric slow crockery cooker, stir together cooked beef, refried beans, taco sauce, olives, and taco seasoning mix. Cover and cook on high-heat setting for 2 hours.

Spoon about 1/4 cup mixture into each taco shell; top with a little lettuce, tomato, and cheese. Pass picante or hot taco sauce.

Old El Paso adds great zest to sandwiches. Here are some flavor-packed tips to add Southwestern pizzazz.

• Sprinkle a spoonful of **Old El Paso Taco Sauce** into a hot beef, corned beef, or meatball sandwich.

• Stir an envelope of **Old El Paso Taco Seasoning Mix** into a pound of ground meat before shaping it into hamburger patties.

• Hide a large square of **Old El Paso Whole Green Chilies** between two thin hamburger patties and form into one large one. Melt some cheese over the top of the cooked burger. Pass **Old El Paso Taco Sauce**.

• Stir some **Old El Paso Taco Sauce** or **Hot Picante Sauce** into the barbecue sauce for ham sandwiches.

• Pass **Old El Paso Taco Sauce** instead of catsup for burgers.

Taco Burgers

1 pound ground beef
1 10-ounce can **Old El Paso Tomatoes and Green Chilies**
1 envelope **Old El Paso Taco Seasoning Mix** ($^1/_3$ cup)
$^1/_4$ cup water
1 tomato, peeled, and chopped
8 hamburger buns, split and toasted
2 cups shredded lettuce
1 cup (4 ounces) shredded American, colby, or Monterey Jack cheese

In skillet, brown the meat; drain off fat. Stir in tomatoes and green chilies, taco seasoning mix, and water. Bring to boiling; reduce heat. Boil gently, uncovered, till thick, about 15 minutes. Stir in tomato; heat through. Spoon onto toasted buns. Sprinkle each of the burgers with lettuce and shredded cheese. Makes 8 servings.

Salad Burritos

$^1/_2$ cup salad oil
3 tablespoons vinegar
$^1/_2$ envelope (about 2 tablespoons) **Old El Paso Taco Seasoning Mix**
$^1/_2$ teaspoon sugar
. . .
1 8-ounce can **Old El Paso Garbanzos**, drained
$^1/_2$ cup sliced pitted ripe olives
$^1/_2$ small onion, cut in rings
. . .
8 ounces Monterey Jack cheese, cut in strips
1 small head lettuce, torn
1 **Old El Paso Whole Green Chili** seeded, rinsed, and sliced in thin strips
12 8-inch flour tortillas
1 12-ounce jar **Old El Paso Mexi Pickles**

In a screw-top jar, combine salad oil, vinegar, dry taco seasoning mix, and sugar. Cover and shake well.
  Combine garbanzo beans, olives, and onion rings; pour salad dressing over and toss. Chill.
  Place cheese, lettuce, and chili atop marinated salad; toss. Spoon about $^1/_2$ cup salad atop each tortilla; roll up, folding in sides. Serve with Mexi pickles. Makes 6 servings.

Burritos

12 8-inch flour tortillas
1 large onion, chopped
2 tablespoons cooking oil
2 16-ounce cans **Old El Paso Refried Beans**
1 large tomato, chopped
3 cups (12 ounces) shredded cheddar cheese
1 cup shredded lettuce
1 medium avocado, seeded, peeled, and cut in 12 wedges
  Old El Paso Taco Sauce

Wrap stack of tortillas tightly in foil; heat in 350° oven for 15 minutes. Cook onion in hot oil till tender but not brown. Add refried beans; cook and stir till heated through. Lightly salt tomato. Spoon about $^1/_3$ cup bean mixture onto each tortilla near one edge. Top with cheese, lettuce, tomato, and avocado wedge. Fold edge nearest filling up and over filling just till mixture is covered. Fold in two sides envelope fashion, then roll up. Arrange on baking sheet; bake in 350° oven for 15 minutes or till heated through. Pass taco sauce. Makes 12 burritos.

Meal-In-A-Bowl Soups

Pork Sparerib Soup
Pictured at lower right

2 pounds pork spareribs, cut in half crosswise
1 envelope **Old El Paso Chili Seasoning Mix** (¹/₃ cup)
8 cups water
3 carrots, sliced
2 medium turnips, peeled and quartered
1 large onion, chopped (1 cup)
1¹/₂ teaspoons salt
1 small head cabbage, shredded (4 cups)

Cut ribs apart between bones into individual ribs. Rub each with some of the chili seasoning mix. Reserve any remaining mix. Arrange ribs in shallow baking pan. Bake in 450° oven for 25 minutes or till well browned. Pour off fat. Transfer the browned ribs to 5-quart Dutch oven. Add water, carrots, turnips, onion, any remaining seasoning mix, and salt. Bring mixture to boiling. Reduce heat; cover and simmer for 2 hours or till meat is very tender. Skim off fat. Stir shredded cabbage into soup; cook 5 minutes more. Makes 6 servings.

Tortilla-Ball Soup
Pictured at upper right

10 **Old El Paso Tortillas,** torn
¹/₄ cup milk
1 small onion, cut up
1 clove garlic
1 egg
¹/₂ teaspoon salt
¹/₈ teaspoon pepper
1 4-ounce can **Old El Paso Whole Green Chilies,** seeded, rinsed, and chopped
¹/₄ cup (1 ounce) shredded cheddar or Monterey Jack cheese
Cooking oil
3 cups beef broth
¹/₂ cup light cream
2 tablespoons **Old El Paso Taco Sauce**

Place tortillas and milk in blender container; let stand 5 minutes. Add onion, garlic, egg, salt, and pepper. Cover and blend till mixture is smooth. Turn mixture into bowl; fold in chilies and cheese. Shape mixture into 18 one-inch balls using about 1 tablespoon mixture for each. Fry tortilla balls in ¹/₂ inch hot oil 1¹/₂ minutes or till lightly browned, turning once. Drain on paper toweling. Keep warm.

In saucepan, combine beef broth, cream, and taco sauce. Heat through.* Sprinkle with cilantro or parsley leaves, if desired. Add tortilla balls; serve immediately. Makes 6 servings.

*Taste for seasoning; add additional taco sauce, if desired.

Garbanzo Hot Pot

1 cup chopped onion
2 tablespoons butter or margarine
2 15-ounce cans **Old El Paso Garbanzos,** drained
1 13³/₄-ounce can chicken broth
1 cup chopped, peeled tomato
¹/₄ cup **Old El Paso Chopped Green Chilies**
¹/₂ teaspoon salt
¹/₄ teaspoon dried marjoram leaves, crushed
¹/₈ teaspoon pepper
1 bay leaf

In large skillet, cook onion in butter or margarine till tender but not brown. Stir in garbanzos, chicken broth, tomato, chilies, salt, marjoram, pepper, and bay leaf. Reduce heat; simmer, uncovered, 20 minutes. Remove bay leaf before serving. Makes 4 or 5 servings.

Bean Soup and Tamale Dumplings

Pictured at right. For a super zesty soup use half a package of chili seasoning mix in the meat mixture and the other half in the soup.

½ pound ground beef
¼ cup chopped onion
1 tablespoon **Old El Paso Chili Seasoning Mix**
1½ cups yellow cornmeal
¾ cup all-purpose flour
2 teaspoons baking powder
1 teaspoon salt
1 teaspoon sugar
1 cup water
6 slices bacon, chopped
1 cup chopped onion
1 clove garlic, minced
1 tablespoon **Old El Paso Chili Seasoning Mix**
4 cups water
1 tablespoon instant beef bouillon granules
2 15-ounce cans **Old El Paso Mexe-Beans**

To make *Tamale Dumplings:* In skillet, cook ground beef and the ¼ cup chopped onion till meat is brown and onion is tender. Drain off excess fat. Stir in the first 1 tablespoon chili seasoning mix; set aside to cool.

In bowl, combine cornmeal, flour, baking powder, salt, and sugar. Add the 1 cup water, stirring till mixture is combined. Divide cornmeal mixture into 16 portions. With lightly floured hands, shape each portion around a teaspoonful of meat mixture to form a ball. Reserve any remaining meat mixture.

In Dutch oven, cook together bacon, the remaining 1 cup chopped onion, and garlic till onion is tender. Stir in the remaining 1 tablespoon chili seasoning mix, the 4 cups water, and the bouillon granules. Stir in Mexe-beans and the remaining meat mixture. Bring to boiling; reduce heat to simmer. Add *Tamale Dumplings.* Cover tightly; simmer 20 minutes. Makes 6 to 8 servings.

Hearty Hodgepodge

1 medium onion, thinly sliced
2 tablespoons cooking oil
1 1-pound beef shank
1 ¾-pound ham hock
6 cups water
2 teaspoons salt
2 15-ounce cans **Old El Paso Garbanzos**
3 cups diced, peeled potatoes (4 medium)
1 clove garlic, minced
1 4-ounce link Polish sausage, thinly sliced

In Dutch oven, cook onion in hot oil till tender but not brown. Add beef shank, ham hock, water, and salt. Cover; simmer 1½ hours. Remove meat from bones; dice. Skim fat from broth. Stir in meat, beans, potatoes, and garlic. Cover and simmer 30 minutes more. Add sausage. Simmer, covered, 15 minutes more. Makes 10 servings.

Stir Southwestern Flavor into a Soup. Open a can of soup and let your zesty imagination run wild. Top a bowl of steamy hot soup with one of the following:
• Add a spoonful of **Old El Paso Taco** or **Picante Sauce** to a bowl of tomato soup.
• Stir some **Old El Paso Garbanzos** or **Mexe-Beans** into a vegetable soup or a turkey chowder.
• Dollop a touch of **Old El Paso Jalapeño Relish** into a bowl of beef-vegetable soup.
• Slice **Old El Paso Tamales** into a bean or pea soup.
• Add contrast to minestrone with a little **Old El Paso Jalapeño Sauce**.

Stack-Up El Paso Dinners

Tuna Tostadas

Pictured on page 7

- 1 tablespoon lime juice
- ¼ teaspoon salt
  Dash pepper
- 1 9¼-ounce can tuna, drained and flaked **or** 7½-ounce can crabmeat, drained, flaked, and cartilage removed
- 2 **Old El Paso Whole Green Chilies**, seeded, rinsed, and chopped
- 8 **Old El Paso Tostada Shells**
- 1 small avocado
- 2 cups shredded lettuce
- 1 tomato, chopped and drained
  Lime wedges
  Old El Paso Taco Sauce

In bowl, combine lime juice, salt, and pepper; toss with tuna and chilies. Divide mixture among tostada shells. Seed, peel, and cube avocado. Top tuna with lettuce, tomato, and avocado. Pass lime wedges and taco sauce. Makes 8 servings.

Chicken Tostadas

Pictured at right

- 8 **Old El Paso Tostada Shells**
- 2 medium chicken breasts, skinned, boned, and cut in thin strips
- ¼ cup sliced green onion
- 2 tablespoons butter or margarine
- 1 8-ounce can tomato sauce
- 1 envelope **Old El Paso Taco Seasoning Mix** (⅓ cup)
- 2 cups shredded lettuce
- 2 medium tomatoes, chopped
- 1 cup (4 ounces) shredded Monterey Jack cheese
  Avocado slices
  Old El Paso Taco Sauce

Heat tostada shells according to package directions; keep warm. In medium skillet, quickly cook chicken strips and sliced green onion in butter till chicken is browned. Add tomato sauce and taco seasoning mix. Reduce heat and simmer, covered, about 10 minutes.

To assemble tostadas, place warm tostada shells on plate; spoon on chicken mixture. Top with shredded lettuce, chopped tomato, cheese, and avocado slices. Drizzle with taco sauce. Makes 8 servings.

Saucy Beef Tostadas

- 12 **Old El Paso Tostada Shells**
- 1 pound ground beef
- ½ cup chopped onion
- 1 10-ounce can **Old El Paso Tomatoes and Green Chilies**
- 1 envelope **Old El Paso Taco Seasoning Mix** (⅓ cup)
- 1 16-ounce can **Old El Paso Refried Beans**
- 2 tomatoes, cored and chopped
- 2 cups shredded lettuce
- 1 cup (4 ounces) shredded sharp cheddar cheese
  Old El Paso Taco Sauce

Warm tostada shells according to package directions; keep warm. In medium skillet, cook beef and onion till meat is brown and onion is tender; drain off excess fat. Stir in tomatoes and green chilies and taco seasoning mix. Simmer, uncovered, 15 minutes. Heat refried beans.

To assemble tostadas, place warm shells on serving plate. Spread each with warm refried beans. Spoon about ¼ cup meat mixture over refried beans on each tostada shell. Top with tomato, lettuce, and shredded cheese. Pass taco sauce. Makes 12 servings.

Sombrero Salads

Taco Salad

To short cut the hot meat mixture, heat two cans **Old El Paso Chili with Beans** and pour over the tossed salad. Keep the chili on the pantry shelf for this tasty and quick-to-fix main dish salad. Your drop-in guests will love it.

1 pound ground beef
1 envelope **Old El Paso Taco Seasoning Mix** (¹/₃ cup)
³/₄ cup water
. . .
1 medium head lettuce, torn in bite-size pieces (4 cups)
¹/₂ cup sliced ripe olives
1 cup (4 ounces) shredded sharp cheddar cheese
1 large tomato, cut in wedges
1 small onion, thinly sliced and separated in rings
Avocado slices
Coarsely crushed **Old El Paso Taco** or **Tostada Shells**
Old El Paso Taco Sauce

In skillet, cook ground meat till brown; drain off excess fat. Stir in taco seasoning mix and water. Bring to boiling; reduce heat and simmer, uncovered, 15 to 20 minutes, stirring occasionally.

In salad bowl, combine lettuce, olives and cheese; toss well. Top with meat mixture, tomato, onion, avocado slices, and broken taco shells. Pass taco sauce. Makes 4 to 6 servings.

Cauliflower Salad

1 medium head cauliflower
. . .
2 cups Guacamole (see page 10)
¹/₂ cup (2 ounces) shredded Monterey Jack or cheddar cheese
Radish roses

Remove leaves and core from cauliflower. In covered saucepan, cook whole cauliflower in small amount of boiling salted water 20 to 25 minutes or till just tender when tested with a fork. Drain well and chill. Place chilled cauliflower on platter. Spread Guacamole over entire surface. Sprinkle with cheese. Garnish platter with radish roses. Makes 6 to 8 servings.

Three Bean Salad

1 15-ounce can **Old El Paso Garbanzos**, drained
1 15-ounce can **Old El Paso Pinto Beans**, drained
1 15-ounce can cut green beans, drained
1 small onion, sliced
¹/₂ cup chopped celery
. . .
¹/₄ cup sugar
¹/₄ cup vinegar
¹/₄ cup salad oil
1 teaspoon salt
¹/₄ teaspoon pepper
2 **Old El Paso Pickled Chilies Jalapeños**, seeded, rinsed and chopped (optional)

In large bowl, combine garbanzos, pinto beans, green beans, onion, and celery. Combine sugar, vinegar, oil, salt, pepper, and jalapeños, if desired; mix well. Pour dressing over vegetables and toss. Cover and chill at least 4 hours, stirring occasionally. Makes 6 servings.

Great Southwest Burgers

Tostada Burger

1 beaten egg
1/2 cup crushed **Old El Paso Taco or Tostada Shells**
1/4 cup water
1 envelope **Old El Paso Taco Seasoning Mix** (1/3 cup)
1 pound ground beef

4 hamburger buns, toasted
1 8-ounce can tomato sauce

1 large tomato, sliced
1 cup shredded lettuce
1/2 cup (2 ounces) shredded sharp cheddar cheese

In mixing bowl, combine egg, crushed taco shells, water, and *half* the package of seasoning mix. Add meat; mix well. Shape meat mixture into 4 patties. Cook over medium coals 5 to 6 minutes. Turn; cook 4 to 5 minutes more or till of desired doneness. Serve on buns. Combine tomato sauce and the remaining taco seasoning mix; spoon some atop the burgers. Pass tomato, lettuce, and cheese. Makes 4 servings.

Fiesta Burgers

3 beaten eggs
1 7½-ounce can **Old El Paso Taco Sauce**
1½ cups soft bread crumbs (2 slices bread)
1 4-ounce can **Old El Paso Whole Green Chilies**, seeded, rinsed, and chopped
1½ teaspoons salt
3 pounds ground beef

12 hamburger buns, split, toasted, and buttered

In bowl, combine eggs, taco sauce, bread crumbs, chilies, and salt. Add ground beef; mix well. Shape meat mixture into 12 patties. Grill over medium coals for 8 to 9 minutes. Turn and grill till of desired doneness. (For medium, grill 7 more minutes.) Serve in buns. Makes 12 servings.

Beef and Bean Burritos

1 cup **Old El Paso Refried Beans** (1/2 of a 16-ounce can)
1 4-ounce can **Old El Paso Whole Green Chilies**, seeded, rinsed, and chopped
1/4 cup chopped onion
3/4 teaspoon salt
1½ pounds ground beef
4 slices sharp American cheese

8 8-inch flour tortillas
1 cup chopped lettuce
1 medium tomato, chopped

Combine beans, 2 tablespoons of the chilies, onion, and salt. Add beef; mix well. Form into eight 5-inch patties. Cut cheese slices in half; place 1/2 cheese slice on each beef patty. Fold to seal cheese inside, forming a semicircle. Grill over medium coals for 5 to 6 minutes; turn and grill 4 to 5 minutes more. Heat the tortillas on grill. Serve burgers in hot tortillas. Add lettuce, chopped tomato, and the remaining chili peppers as desired. Makes 8 servings.

Guacamole Burgers

Guacamole Burgers

Pictured above

- 1 pound ground beef
- ½ cup crushed **Old El Paso Taco or Tostada Shells**
- ⅓ cup milk
- ½ teaspoon onion salt
- 1 small tomato, peeled, seeded, and chopped
- 1 cup Guacamole (see page 10)
- 5 hamburger buns, split, toasted, and buttered

Mix together ground beef, crushed taco shells, milk, and onion salt. Shape into 5 patties. Grill over hot coals 4 to 5 minutes on each side.

Stir tomato into Guacamole. Top each burger with Guacamole; serve in buns. Makes 5 servings.

RIO GRANDE ENTERTAINING

Sundown Appetizers

Sunrise Nuggets

Pictured at top of photo

8 ounces lean ground meat
1 8¼-ounce can (1 cup) **Old El Paso Refried Beans**
2 tablespoons **Old El Paso Taco Sauce**

. . .

2 to 4 tablespoons cooking oil

. . .

Guacamole (see page 10)
Radish slices

Thoroughly combine ground meat, refried beans, and taco sauce; chill 30 minutes. Shape mixture into 16 patties, 1½-inches in diameter. In skillet, fry nuggets in hot fat till brown on both sides, about 4 minutes per side. Drain on paper toweling. Top each with 1 tablespoon Guacamole and a radish slice. Makes 16 appetizers.

Vegetable-Filled Turnovers

Pictured at lower left of photo

2 cups all-purpose flour
1½ teaspoons baking powder
1 teaspoon salt
½ cup shortening or lard
⅓ cup cold water

. . .

Fat for frying (optional)
Milk (optional)

. . .

1 small zucchini
1 large tomato
½ of a 4-ounce can **Old El Paso Chopped Green Chilies**
¾ cup (3 ounces) shredded cheddar cheese

In bowl, stir together flour, baking powder, and salt. Cut in shortening till mixture resembles cornmeal. Add the cold water, a little at a time, stirring with fork till dough forms a ball. Divide into 20 portions. On floured surface, roll each piece of dough to a 4-inch circle. Place about 1 tablespoon *Vegetable Filling* on each. Moisten edges with a little water; fold in half, pressing edges with fork to seal. Fry in 1½ inches hot fat (375°) for 3 minutes or till golden, turning once. Drain on paper toweling. (Or, place on baking sheet; brush with milk. Bake in 425° oven 15 to 18 minutes or till golden.) Makes 20 appetizers.

To Make Vegetable Filling: Trim ends from zucchini; cook whole zucchini, covered, in small amount of boiling salted water for 10 minutes or till tender. Drain and chop. Peel, seed, and chop tomato; sprinkle with a little salt. Combine with zucchini, chilies, and cheese. Makes about 2 cups.

Southwest Tarts

Pictured lower right

1 2-crust-size package pastry mix

. . .

1 medium tomato
1 4-ounce can **Old El Paso Chopped Green Chilies**
1 cup chopped cooked chicken
1 teaspoon vinegar
½ teaspoon salt
½ cup dairy sour cream
½ cup sliced pitted ripe olives

Prepare pastry mix according to package directions; divide in 24 portions. On floured surface roll each portion to a 5x3-inch oval or a 4-inch round. Place each on piece of aluminum foil about the same size. Fold up foil and pinch edge of dough to form a rim. Place on baking sheet and bake in 375° oven for 10 to 12 minutes. Remove and cool on wire rack. Discard foil. Fill each with *Chicken Filling:* Peel and chop tomato; stir in chilies and chicken. Add vinegar and salt. Chill till ready to fill. Top with sour cream and olives. Makes 2 dozen appetizers.

Cheese Nachos

Pictured on page 47

Old El Paso Tostada Shells,
  broken in sixths
Monterey Jack or cheddar cheese
Old El Paso Whole Green Chilies,
  seeded and rinsed

Spread broken tostada shells in a single layer on an ovenproof plate or baking sheet. Cut cheese in $3/4$x $3/4$x$1/4$-inch pieces. Cut chili pepper in strips. Place a piece of cheese on each shell; top with strip of chili. Bake in 400° oven for 5 minutes or till cheese melts. Serve hot.
Microwave Directions: Prepare Cheese Nachos as above. Place 12 on plate. Micro-cook, uncovered, on high power, just till cheese melts, 30 to 45 seconds, turning plate several times. Repeat in units of 12.

Cheese Turnovers

 6 ounces Monterey Jack cheese
 1 4-ounce can **Old El Paso Whole Green Chilies,** seeded and rinsed
$3/4$ cup **Old El Paso Refried Beans**
12 **Old El Paso Tortillas**
        · · ·
 2 tablespoons cooking oil

Cut cheese into twelve 3x1x$1/4$-inch strips. Quarter chilies lengthwise. Spread 1 tablespoon of the beans on each tortilla. Top each with a piece of cheese and a piece of chili. Fold tortillas in half; secure each with a wooden pick. In skillet, heat oil; cook turnovers, a few at a time, in the hot oil about 2 minutes per side or till lightly browned and cheese is melted. Makes 12 appetizers.

Chilies-Cheese Stuffed Eggs

 6 hard-cooked eggs
$1/4$ cup process cheese spread
 2 tablespoons **Old El Paso Chopped Green Chilies**
   Dash salt
   Paprika

Halve eggs lengthwise. Remove yolks; mash. Blend yolks with cheese spread, chilies, and salt. Refill whites; sprinkle with paprika. Chill. Makes 12.

Enchilada Bites

Make ahead and refrigerate. These tasty tidbits need only 20 minutes in the oven.

 2 cups crumbled cornbread
 1 10-ounce can **Old El Paso Mild Enchilada Sauce**
$1/2$ teaspoon salt
$1/2$ pounds ground beef
        · · ·
 1 8-ounce can tomato sauce
$1/2$ cup (2 ounces) shredded Monterey Jack cheese

Combine cornbread crumbs, $1/2$ cup of the enchilada sauce, and the salt. Add ground beef; mix well. Shape into 1-inch balls. Place in shallow baking pan. Bake, uncovered, in 350° oven for 18 to 20 minutes or till done. Meanwhile, in small saucepan, heat together tomato sauce and the remaining enchilada sauce. Place cooked meat balls in chafing dish; pour sauce over and top with shredded cheese. Keep warm over low heat. Serve with wooden picks. Makes about 90 appetizers.

Cheese and Chilies

8 eggs
½ cup all-purpose flour
1 teaspoon baking powder
¾ teaspoon salt

. . .

3 cups (12 ounces) shredded
  Monterey Jack cheese
1½ cups (12 ounces) cream-style
  cottage cheese
2 4-ounce cans **Old El Paso Whole
  Green Chilies**, seeded, rinsed,
  and chopped

In large mixer bowl, beat eggs with electric mixer till light, 4 to 5 minutes. Stir together flour, baking powder, and salt. Add to eggs and mix well. Fold in Monterey Jack cheese, cottage cheese, and chilies. Turn into greased 9x9x2-inch baking dish. Bake in 350° oven for 40 minutes. Remove from oven; let stand 10 minutes. Cut in small squares; serve warm. Makes 3 to 4 dozen appetizers.

Texas Spread

2 cups (8 ounces) shredded sharp
  cheddar cheese
¼ cup milk

. . .

2 tablespoons butter or margarine
1 clove garlic, minced
½ cup **Old El Paso Chopped Green
  Chilies**

. . .

Crackers

Bring cheddar cheese to room temperature. Heat milk to boiling; pour over cheese in mixer bowl. Beat with electric mixer till nearly smooth. Add butter and garlic; beat well. Stir in chopped chilies. (Mixture will be thin.) Chill well. Serve with crackers. Makes 1½ cups spread.

Hominy Rounds

2 15-ounce cans hominy, drained
1 teaspoon salt
  Fat for frying

. . .

1 16-ounce can **Old El Paso Refried
  Beans**
1 cup mashed avocado
1 cup dairy sour cream

In large bowl, combine hominy and salt. Mash till consistency of mush. With hands, shape into rounds 1½ inches in diameter and ½ inch thick. In skillet, fry rounds in small amount of hot fat about 1 minute on each side or till golden. Drain on paper toweling. Meanwhile, heat refried beans. Top each round with some of the refried beans, the avocado, and sour cream. Makes about 20 appetizers.

Hot Bean Dipper

1 16-ounce can **Old El Paso Refried
  Beans**
1 11-ounce can condensed cheddar
  cheese soup
¼ cup milk
3 tablespoons **Old El Paso Chopped
  Green Chilies**

. . .

Old El Paso Tostada Shells,
  broken

In saucepan, combine beans, soup, milk, and chilies. Heat slowly, stirring constantly, till smooth and bubbly. Transfer to fondue pot; place over fondue burner. Use broken tostada shells as dippers. Makes 3 cups.

Yucatan Shrimp Appetizer

1 cup coarsely chopped seeded
    tomato
1/2 cup finely chopped onion
1/4 cup snipped cilantro or parsley
1 to 2 tablespoons finely chopped
    Old El Paso Hot Green Chili
    Peppers
2 tablespoons cooking oil
2 tablespoons lime juice
1/2 teaspoon salt
    Dash pepper
    . . .
1 cup shredded lettuce
1 pound fresh or frozen shelled
    large shrimp, cooked and
    chilled

Combine tomato, onion, cilantro, chili peppers, oil, lime juice, salt, and pepper. Cover; chill. Place lettuce in 8 cocktail glasses; arrange shrimp atop. Spoon tomato mixture over shrimp. Makes 8 servings.

Hot Bean and Cheese Dip

1 11 1/2-ounce can condensed bean
    with bacon soup
1 cup (4 ounces) shredded sharp
    American cheese
1/4 cup **Old El Paso Chopped Green**
    Chilies
1 teaspoon instant minced onion
    Dash garlic powder
1/4 cup water
    . . .
    Old El Paso Tostada Shells,
    broken

In saucepan, combine soup, cheese, chilies, onion, garlic powder, and water. Heat slowly, stirring constantly, till heated through. Transfer to fondue pot or small chafing dish. Keep warm over fondue or chafing dish burner. Add water to thin, as necessary. Serve with tostada shells for dippers. Makes about 2 cups dip.

Mexican Fondue

1 10-ounce can **Old El Paso Mild**
    Enchilada Sauce
1/4 cup **Old El Paso Chopped Green**
    Chilies
3 cups (12 ounces) shredded
    muenster cheese
1/4 teaspoon chili powder
1 teaspoon cornstarch
1 tablespoon cold water
    . . .
    French bread
    Cooked ham, cubed
    Cooked peeled shrimp

In saucepan, heat enchilada sauce and chilies. Add cheese, a little at a time, stirring till cheese melts. Stir in chili powder. Combine cornstarch and water; add to sauce mixture. Cook and stir till thickened and bubbly. Turn into fondue pot. Keep warm. Serve with French bread, ham, and shrimp for dipping. Makes about 3 cups sauce.

Taco Chicken Wings

The microwave version uses fine dry bread crumbs in place of the crushed taco shells.

1/2 cup all-purpose flour
1 envelope **Old El Paso Taco Seasoning Mix** (1/3 cup)
3 pounds chicken wings, tips removed and cut at joints (about 32 chicken pieces)
6 tablespoons butter or margarine
1 cup finely crushed **Old El Paso Taco or Tostada Shells**

In paper or plastic bag, combine flour and taco seasoning mix. Add 2 or 3 chicken pieces at a time; shake to coat. Melt butter in 15x10x1-inch baking pan. Place chicken in pan, turning once to butter surfaces, then roll in taco shells and return to pan. Bake in 350° oven for 40 to 45 minutes. Makes about 32 appetizers.

Microwave Directions: Prepare 1 1/2 pounds of chicken wings at a time. Dip the 16 chicken pieces in a little milk. In paper or plastic bag, combine half a package of the taco seasoning mix with 2 tablespoons fine dry *bread crumbs*. Add two or three chicken pieces at a time, shaking to coat. Place chicken in 12x7 1/2x2-inch baking dish. Micro-cook, covered, on high power, till chicken is done, about 14 minutes, giving dish half turns every 4 minutes.

Mariachi Dips and Nibbles

Easy Cheese Ball

2 8-ounce packages cream cheese, softened
1/2 cup butter or margarine, softened
1/4 cup milk
1 envelope **Old El Paso Taco Seasoning Mix** (1/3 cup)
1/2 teaspoon caraway seed
Radish slices

In small mixer bowl, beat together cream cheese and butter or margarine. Gradually blend in milk, then gradually beat in seasoning mix. Stir in caraway seed. Line small bowl with clear plastic wrap; turn cheese mixture into bowl. Chill 3 to 4 hours. Invert onto serving plate; remove plastic wrap and smooth surface with spatula. Serve with radish slices and garnish with parsley, if desired. Makes 2 3/4 cups.

Nachos

4 ounces cheddar cheese
8 **Old El Paso Tostada Shells,** broken in sixths
1 cup **Old El Paso Refried Beans** (1/2 of a 16-ounce can) **or** 1 10 1/2-ounce container **Old El Paso Jalapeño Bean Dip**
2 **Old El Paso Whole Green Chilies** or **Pickled Chilies Jalapeños,** seeded, rinsed, and cut in thin strips

Cut cheese in 48 pieces, each measuring 3/4x3/4x1/8 inch. Arrange broken tostada shells on baking sheets. Place a teaspoon of refried beans or of bean dip in center of each tostada shell. Top beans with a piece of cheese and of chili. Broil 4 inches from heat till cheese begins to melt, 1 to 3 minutes. Makes 4 dozen.

Shrimp-Cucumber Dip

1 medium unpared cucumber
1 cup cream-style cottage cheese, drained
2 tablespoons finely chopped onion
2 to 4 tablespoons **Old El Paso Jalapeño Relish**
1 4 1/2-ounce can shrimp, drained and chopped

Cut cucumber in half lengthwise; remove seeds and discard. Shred enough cucumber to make 1 cup; drain. In small mixer bowl, combine shredded cucumber, drained cottage cheese, and onion; beat till nearly smooth. Blend in relish; stir in shrimp. Chill before serving. Garnish with additional shrimp, if desired. Serve with crackers or celery and carrot sticks. Makes about 2 cups.

Clamavo Dip

2 ripe avocados, seeded, peeled, and cut into pieces
1 7 1/2-ounce can minced clams, drained
1 4-ounce can **Old El Paso Taco Sauce**
1 or 2 **Old El Paso Pickled Chilies Jalapeños,** rinsed, seeded, and chopped (optional)
2 tablespoons mayonnaise or salad dressing
1/2 teaspoon salt

In blender container or small mixer bowl, combine all ingredients. Beat or blend till smooth. Chill to blend flavors. Use crackers or **Old El Paso Tostada Shells,** broken into quarters, for dippers. Garnish with onion rings, if desired. Makes 1 2/3 cups.

Confetti Cheese Dip

1/2 cup finely chopped onion
1 tablespoon butter or margarine
2 medium tomatoes, peeled, seeded, cored, and chopped
1 4-ounce can **Old El Paso Whole Green Chilies**, seeded, rinsed, and chopped
1/4 teaspoon salt

. . .

1 1/2 cups (6 ounces) shredded cheddar cheese
Milk
Old El Paso Tostada Shells, broken

In medium skillet, cook onion in butter or margarine till tender but not brown. Stir in tomatoes, chilies, and salt. Simmer, uncovered, for 10 minutes. Add cheese, a little at a time, stirring till cheese is melted. Stir in a little milk if mixture becomes too thick. Serve immediately with tostada shells for dippers. Makes 1 3/4 cups dip.

Mexi-Bean Dunk

1 cup cream-style cottage cheese
1 15-ounce can **Old El Paso Mexe-Beans**, drained and rinsed
1 envelope **Old El Paso Chili Seasoning Mix** (1/3 cup)
Old El Paso Tostada Shells, broken

In blender container, blend cottage cheese at low speed till smooth. Add Mexe-beans and chili seasoning mix. Cover and blend at low speed till combined, stopping blender to scrape down sides once or twice. Blend at high speed till mixture is nearly smooth, a few seconds more. Serve with broken tostada shells for dippers. Makes 2 cups dip.

Border-Town Dip

For added zest, stir in a little **Old El Paso Jalapeño Relish**.

1 cup **Old El Paso Refried Beans** (1/2 of a 16-ounce can)
1/2 cup (2 ounces) shredded provolone cheese
1/3 cup beer *or* water
2 tablespoons butter or margarine
1 tablespoon minced onion
1 clove garlic, minced
2 teaspoons chili powder
Old El Paso Tostada Shells, broken

In saucepan, combine beans, cheese, beer or water, butter or margarine, onion, garlic, and chili powder. Heat and stir till hot through, 5 to 10 minutes. Transfer to small fondue pot. Serve with broken tostada shells. Makes 1 1/4 cups dip.

Make your own Chip Dippers. Give dips added Mexican flair and serve them with chips made from **Old El Paso Tortillas** *or* **Tostada Shells.**

For tortillas, stack and cut into six wedges. In heavy saucepan or deep skillet, heat 1/2 inch cooking oil or shortening. Fry the tortilla wedges, a few at a time, about 1 minute or till they are crisp and lightly browned. Drain well on paper toweling. Sprinkle lightly with a little salt.

For tostada shells, simply break the shells into fourths or sixths and serve them as dippers.

Peppy Bean Dip

For an extra speedy dip, heat up a can of **Old El Paso Refried Beans, Refried Beans with Sausage, Tomatoes and Green Chilies**, or **Jalapeño Relish** and serve with tortilla chips or broken **Old El Paso Tostada Shells**. For a peppier version, try the recipe below.

1 16-ounce can **Old El Paso Refried Beans**
1 cup dairy sour cream
3 to 5 **Old El Paso Pickled Chilies Jalapeños**, seeded and rinsed

· · ·

Shredded cheddar cheese
Sliced green onion
Old El Paso Tostada Shells, broken

Blend together refried beans and sour cream. Finely chop the jalapeño peppers; mix well with bean mixture. Spoon into serving bowl; garnish with shredded cheddar cheese and sliced green onion, if desired. Serve with broken tostada shells for dippers. Makes about 2³/₄ cups dip.

Fiesta Dinners

Hominy Stew

Pictured at right in back

1½ pounds beef stew meat, cut in
    ½-inch pieces
  4 cups water
½ cup chopped onion
1½ teaspoons salt

       . . .

  2 15-ounce cans hominy, drained
  1 10-ounce can **Old El Paso
    Tomatoes and Green Chilies**

       . . .

½ cup cold water
¼ cup all-purpose flour
  Shredded cabbage
  Sliced green onion
  Sliced radish

In 3-quart saucepan, combine beef, the 4 cups water, the chopped onion, and the salt. Cover; simmer 1½ hours. Add hominy and tomatoes and green chilies. Cover; simmer 30 minutes more. Blend the cold water into the flour; add to beef mixture. Cook and stir till thickened and bubbly. Serve in bowls; top with cabbage, green onion, and radish. Makes 6 to 8 servings.

Studded Pot Roast

  1 3-pound beef brisket
  5 slices bacon, cut up
  2 tablespoons slivered almonds
  2 tablespoons cooking oil

       . . .

¾ cup water
  1 4-ounce can **Old El Paso Chopped
    Green Chilies**
  2 tablespoons vinegar
  2 cloves garlic, minced
  1 teaspoon salt
¼ teaspoon ground cinnamon
¼ teaspoon dried thyme, crushed
¼ teaspoon dried marjoram,
    crushed
¼ teaspoon dried oregano, crushed
⅛ teaspoon ground cloves
⅛ teaspoon pepper

       . . .

  4 large potatoes, peeled and cut in
    pieces

Trim visible fat from brisket. Cut small slits about 1 inch deep in top surface of meat and stud with raw bacon pieces and slivered almonds. In large Dutch oven, brown studded brisket on both sides in hot cooking oil.

Combine water, chopped chilies, vinegar, garlic, salt, cinnamon, thyme, marjoram, oregano, cloves, and pepper. Pour chili mixture over meat. Cover; simmer for 1 hour and 45 minutes. Add potatoes and, if needed, more water. Cover; simmer 45 minutes more or till potatoes are tender. Makes 6 servings.

Chilies Relleños

Relleños, "ray-LYAY-nos," means stuffed

  6 **Old El Paso Whole Green Chilies**
  2 cups (8 ounces) shredded sharp
    cheddar cheese
    All-purpose flour
  6 egg whites
  3 tablespoons all-purpose flour
    Dash salt
  6 egg yolks
    Shortening or cooking oil

Slit chilies lengthwise; seed. Stuff peppers with cheese; roll in a little flour. Beat egg whites till stiff but not dry. Add 3 tablespoons all-purpose flour and salt to egg yolks; beat till thick and lemon-colored. Fold into whites.

In skillet at least 3 inches deep, heat 1 inch fat to 375°. For each Chili Relleño, spoon ¼ cup batter into hot fat, spreading into a circle. As batter begins to set, gently top with a pepper. Cover with more batter. Continue cooking till browned, turning once; drain on paper toweling. Serve at once. Makes 6 servings.

Guacamole (recipe page 10), Hominy Stew, and Tortilla Skillet

Tortilla Skillet

Pictured above

  6 **Old El Paso Tortillas**
    Cooking oil

      . . .

  4 slightly beaten eggs
¼ teaspoon salt
  1 10-ounce can **Old El Paso Mild**
    Enchilada Sauce
1½ cups (6 ounces) crumbled soft
    Mexican or farmer's cheese
½ cup water
¼ cup sliced green onion

Tear tortillas in 1½-inch pieces. Heat ½ inch oil in heavy saucepan or deep skillet. Fry tortilla pieces in hot oil for 45 to 60 seconds or till crisp and golden. Remove with slotted spoon; drain on paper toweling. Pour all but 2 tablespoons oil from skillet; return tortillas to skillet.

Stir in eggs and salt; cook and stir till tortillas are coated and eggs are set. Stir in enchilada sauce, *1 cup* of the cheese, the water, and *half* the onion. Simmer, uncovered, for 15 minutes. Turn into serving dish; top with remaining cheese and onion. Makes 4 servings.

Marinated Raw Fish

Known as Ceviche or Seviche, this delicate first course gets its characteristic flavor and texture from the lime or lemon juice that "cooks" the fish.

 1 pound fresh or frozen haddock
   fillets or other fish fillets
 1 cup fresh lime or lemon juice

     · · ·

 1 small onion
 2 to 3 **Old El Paso Pickled Chilies
   Jalapeños,** seeded, rinsed, and
   cut in strips
¼ cup olive oil or cooking oil
¾ teaspoon salt
¼ teaspoon dried oregano, crushed
⅛ teaspoon pepper
 2 medium tomatoes
   Snipped cilantro or parsley

Thaw frozen fish. Cut fish fillets into ½-inch cubes. In a nonmetal bowl, cover cubed fish with lime or lemon juice. Cover and refrigerate at least 4 hours or till fish is opaque, turning occasionally. Thinly slice the onion; separate into rings. Add to fish with pickled jalapeños, olive oil, salt, oregano, and pepper. Toss gently to combine well; chill.

Peel, seed, and chop tomatoes; toss with chilled fish mixture. Sprinkle with snipped cilantro. Makes 10 to 12 appetizer servings.

Stuffed Jalapeños

These are the ultimate in hotness.

12 **Old El Paso Pickled Chilies
   Jalapeños**
 1 3-ounce package cream cheese,
   softened
½ cup (2 ounces) shredded sharp
   cheddar cheese
¼ cup sliced green onion
12 pimiento strips

Rinse and drain jalapeños. Slit lengthwise on one side; remove seeds and veins, leaving stem attached. Beat cream cheese till fluffy. Beat in cheddar cheese and green onion. Stuff each pepper with part of the cheese mixture. Arrange on heatproof serving plate or baking sheet; bake in 350° oven for 10 minutes or till cheese melts. Top each pepper with a pimiento strip. Makes 12 appetizers.

Throw a Fiesta Dinner. For an interesting Mexican dinner don't spare festive flavors. Try the following menu out on an adventurous group for an exciting evening.

Margaritas
Stuffed Jalapeño Peppers and
Marinated Raw Fish

· · ·

Chicken in Molé Sauce
Mexican Seasoned Rice
Old El Paso Refried Beans
Tomato Slices topped with Guacamole
(recipe page 10)

· · ·

Fresh Pineapple
Coffee

Chicken in Molé Sauce

The blended nuts are the typical thickening for the Molé (mo-lay ′) sauce.

1/3 cup all-purpose flour
1 envelope **Old El Paso Taco Seasoning Mix** (1/3 cup)
2 2½- to 3-pound broiler-fryer chickens, cut up
3 tablespoons cooking oil
1 10-ounce can **Old El Paso Tomatoes and Green Chilies**
1 teaspoon instant chicken bouillon granules
1/2 cup boiling water
1 small onion, cut up
1/4 cup chopped walnuts
1/4 cup blanched almonds
3 sprigs cilantro or parsley

In paper or plastic bag, combine flour and taco seasoning mix. Add 2 or 3 pieces of chicken at a time; shake to coat. In 12-inch skillet, brown chicken pieces in hot oil, half at a time. Return all to skillet. Reduce heat; cover tightly. Cook 35 to 40 minutes more or till chicken is tender, uncovering skillet during last 10 minutes.

For Molé Sauce: In blender container, combine tomatoes and green chilies, bouillon granules dissolved in boiling water, onion, walnuts, almonds, cilantro, 1/4 *teaspoon salt,* and *a dash of pepper.* Cover and blend till smooth. Heat sauce to boiling in saucepan; serve over chicken. Makes 6 to 8 servings.

Brunch With Punch

Green Chili Quiche

During baking the cheese neatly layers under a delightful chili-studded custard layer.

Pastry for 9-inch pie crust

    . . .

3 eggs
1⅓ cups milk or cream
½ teaspoon salt
Dash pepper
¾ cup (3 ounces) shredded cheddar cheese
1 4-ounce can **Old El Paso Whole Green Chilies**, seeded, rinsed, and chopped

Line 9-inch pie plate with pastry, fluting edges high. Carefully line pastry with foil; cover bottom with dried beans. Bake in 400° oven for 10 minutes; remove foil and beans and bake 3 to 4 minutes more or till lightly browned. Reduce oven temperature to 375°.

In bowl, beat together eggs, milk, salt, and pepper. Stir in cheese and green chilies. Pour into cooled pastry shell. Bake in 375° oven for 35 to 40 minutes or till knife inserted just off center comes out clean. Let stand 10 minutes before serving. Makes 6 servings.

Tostada Salad

A refreshing change in salads to compliment egg dishes

2 ripe avocados, seeded, peeled, and mashed (1 cup)
1 tablespoon lime juice
1 tablespoon thinly sliced green onion
¼ cup dairy sour cream
¼ cup **Old El Paso Taco Sauce**
½ teaspoon salt
1 16-ounce can **Old El Paso Refried Beans**
1 teaspoon cooking oil
½ cup (2 ounces) shredded cheddar cheese
6 **Old El Paso Tostada Shells**
3 cups shredded lettuce
1 cup chopped tomato
Sliced avocado

Thoroughly combine mashed avocado, lime juice, and onion; blend in sour cream, taco sauce, and salt till smooth. Chill.

In skillet, heat refried beans in hot oil; add cheese, stirring till melted. Spread about ⅓ cup beans on each tostada shell. Cover with ½ cup lettuce; top with chopped tomato. Spoon a dollop of avocado dressing atop each salad and garnish with an avocado slice. Makes 6 servings.

Taco Biscuits

These warm biscuits are sensational as a dinner bread, too.

¼ cup **Old El Paso Taco Sauce**
¼ cup milk
½ teaspoon instant minced onion

    . . .

2 cups packaged biscuit mix
Melted butter or margarine
2 tablespoons grated parmesan cheese

In small bowl, combine taco sauce, milk, and instant minced onion; let stand 5 minutes. Stir in biscuit mix till dough clings together. Knead gently on lightly floured surface (5 strokes). Roll or pat dough to ½-inch thickness. Cut with 2½-inch biscuit cutter. Brush with melted butter. Sprinkle each with parmesan cheese. Bake on ungreased baking sheet in 450° oven for 8 to 10 minutes. Makes 8 to 10 biscuits.

Huevos Rancheros (Ranch-Style Eggs)

Huevos Rancheros

"Way' bhoas" is Spanish for eggs.

2 tablespoons cooking oil
6 **Old El Paso Tortillas**

. . .

½ cup chopped onion
1 clove garlic, minced
3 large tomatoes, peeled, cored, and chopped
1 4-ounce can **Old El Paso Whole Green Chilies**, seeded, rinsed, and chopped
¼ teaspoon salt
1 tablespoon cooking oil
6 eggs
1 tablespoon water
1 cup (4 ounces) shredded Monterey Jack cheese

In small skillet, heat the 2 tablespoons oil. Holding tortilla with tongs, dip one at a time in hot oil for 5 seconds on each side or till limp. Line 10x6x2-inch baking dish with tortillas. Keep warm.

In same skillet, cook onion and garlic till tender but not brown (add more oil if necessary). Stir in tomatoes, green chilies, and salt. Simmer, uncovered, for 10 minutes. Spoon over tortillas.

In large skillet, heat the 1 tablespoon oil. Carefully break eggs into skillet; sprinkle with a little salt and pepper. When whites are set and edges cooked, add 1 tablespoon water. Cover skillet and cook eggs to desired doneness.

Using a slotted spoon, carefully arrange cooked eggs over sauce in baking dish. Sprinkle with cheese. Place under broiler 1 to 2 minutes to melt cheese. Serve at once. Makes 6 servings.

Sunflower Eggs

1½ cups uncooked fine noodles
    (3 ounces)
  2 tablespoons cooking oil

    . . .

¾ cup chopped onion
  1 clove garlic, minced
  2 10-ounce cans **Old El Paso
    Tomatoes and Green Chilies**
  1 teaspoon sugar
  1 teaspoon salt
¼ teaspoon ground cinnamon
⅛ teaspoon ground cloves

    . . .

  1 tablespoon cooking oil
  6 eggs
  1 tablespoon water
  1 avocado

In medium skillet, cook noodles in the 2 tablespoons hot oil 3 to 4 minutes or till lightly browned; stir constantly. Remove noodles from skillet, reserving oil; set noodles aside.

Cook onion and garlic in reserved oil till tender. Stir in tomatoes and green chilies, sugar, salt, cinnamon, and cloves. Bring to boiling; reduce heat. Boil gently, uncovered, 15 minutes or till slightly thickened, stirring occasionally. (Should measure 1½ cups.)

Meanwhile, cook the browned noodles in large amount of boiling salted water till tender, 7 to 8 minutes; drain well. In skillet, heat the 1 tablespoon oil. Carefully break eggs into skillet; sprinkle with a little salt and pepper. When whites are set and edges cooked, add the 1 tablespoon water. Cover skillet and cook eggs to desired doneness. Combine noodles and *half* the tomato mixture; transfer to platter. With slotted spoon, transfer eggs to atop noodles. Spoon remaining tomato sauce over. Seed, peel, and slice avocado; arrange slices sunburst-fashion over eggs. Makes 6 servings.

Mexican-Style Eggs

  6 **Old El Paso Tortillas,** torn
  2 tablespoons butter or margarine
  3 beaten eggs
  8 ounces ground beef
  1 10-ounce can **Old El Paso Mild
    Enchilada Sauce**
½ cup sliced green onion
½ cup sliced ripe olives
½ cup dairy sour cream
½ cup (2 ounces) shredded
    American cheese

In skillet, fry tortillas in butter or margarine. Push tortillas to edge of skillet, making a well. Add eggs; cook and stir till softly scrambled. Mix in ground beef and enchilada sauce.

Sprinkle onion and olives over top of egg mixture. Cook, covered, over low heat 10 to 15 minutes. Stir in sour cream and cheese. Continue to cook till heated through, but do not boil. Makes 4 servings.

Sangrita

This peppy and unusual tomato-chili cocktail is the Mexican version of the Bloody Mary. However, the liquor is served separately here.

  6 fully ripe tomatoes, peeled,
    seeded, and cut up *or* 1
    28-ounce can tomatoes
  1 cup orange juice
  1 4-ounce can **Old El Paso Whole
    Green Chilies,** seeded and
    rinsed
  1 slice of a medium onion
⅓ cup lime juice
  1 teaspoon sugar
¼ teaspoon salt
    Old El Paso Picante Sauce
    (optional)
    Tequila

In blender container, place undrained tomatoes, orange juice, chilies, onion, lime juice, sugar, and salt. Cover and blend till smooth. Add picante sauce to taste, if desired. Chill tomato mixture.

Serve each person ½ cup chilled tomato mixture and 1 to 2 ounces (2 to 4 tablespoons) tequila in small separate glasses. Makes 8 to 10 servings.

Baked Mexican Eggs

Baked Mexican Eggs
Pictured above

6 slices bacon
1 16-ounce can tomatoes
¼ cup **Old El Paso Chopped Green Chilies**
1 clove garlic, minced
4 eggs
 Old El Paso Tortillas

Cut bacon in small pieces. In skillet, cook bacon slowly till crisp; drain off excess fat. Add tomatoes, chilies, and garlic to bacon in skillet; heat through. Divide among 4 individual baking dishes. Carefully slip one egg atop tomato mixture in each dish. Sprinkle each lightly with salt and pepper. Bake in 325° oven for 20 to 25 minutes or till eggs are set. Top each with a crisp bacon curl, if desired. Pass rolled tortillas. Makes 4 servings.

El Paso Scrambled Eggs

1 10-ounce can **Old El Paso Tomatoes and Green Chilies**
6 slightly beaten eggs
 Dairy sour cream

In 10-inch skillet, heat tomatoes and green chilies over medium heat till bubbly. Pour beaten eggs over sauce in skillet. Cook without stirring over low heat for 1 to 1½ minutes or till mixture begins to set on bottom. Lift and fold eggs with spatula so uncooked part runs to bottom. Continue lifting and folding about 5 minutes more or till eggs are cooked through, but still glossy and moist. Pass sour cream to spoon on top. Makes 3 to 4 servings.

Sun Country Celebrations

Bean-Avocado Salad

Pictured at right

- 2 15-ounce cans **Old El Paso Mexe-Beans,** drained
- 1 15-ounce can **Old El Paso Garbanzos,** drained
- ¼ cup sliced green onion
  Oil and vinegar dressing

  • • •

  Lettuce
- 4 avocados, halved and seeded

Combine Mexe-beans, garbanzo beans, and green onion. Toss with enough oil and vinegar dressing to coat, about ¼ cup. Arrange lettuce on platter or plates; place 8 avocado halves on lettuce. Spoon bean salad atop avocado shells. Makes 8 servings.

Sausage Pop-Over Olé

- 1 pound lean pork sausage
- 1 cup chopped onion
- ¾ teaspoon chili powder
- ½ teaspoon cumin seed
- 1 10-ounce can **Old El Paso Hot Enchilada Sauce**
- 1 8-ounce can tomato sauce
- 8 ounces sliced Monterey Jack cheese

  • • •

- 2 beaten eggs
- 1 cup milk
- 1 tablespoon oil or sausage drippings
- 1 cup all-purpose flour
- ½ teaspoon seasoned salt
- ½ cup grated parmesan cheese

In skillet, cook sausage and onion till meat is brown and onion is tender. Drain off excess fat, reserving 1 tablespoon for Popover Batter, if desired. Stir in chili powder, cumin seed, enchilada sauce, and tomato sauce; simmer 5 minutes. Spread meat mixture in greased 12x7½x2-inch baking dish. Arrange slices of Monterey Jack over top. Bake in 425° oven for 5 minutes.

Meanwhile, prepare **Popover Batter:** In mixer bowl, combine eggs, milk, oil or sausage drippings, flour, and seasoned salt; beat 2 minutes with electric or rotary beater till smooth. Immediately pour Popover Batter over hot cheese and meat mixture, covering completely. Sprinkle with parmesan. Bake 18 to 20 minutes more or till top is puffed and brown. Cut and serve immediately. Makes 4 to 6 servings.

Mexican Flank Steak

Pictured on page 45

- 2 1-pound beef flank steaks
- ½ teaspoon salt
- ⅛ teaspoon garlic salt
- ⅛ teaspoon pepper
- 1 14½-ounce can **Old El Paso Tamales**

  • • •

- 1 teaspoon instant beef bouillon granules
- ¼ cup boiling water
- 1 7½-ounce can **Old El Paso Taco Sauce**

  • • •

- 1 4-ounce can **Old El Paso Whole Green Chilies,** seeded, rinsed, and cut lengthwise in strips
- ½ cup (2 ounces) shredded Monterey Jack cheese

Pound meat on both sides; sprinkle with the salt, garlic salt, and pepper. Unwrap tamales; place tamales in bowl. Break up slightly with fork; spread over steaks. Roll up each from short side as for jelly rolls; tie each with string. Place in 12x7½x2-inch baking pan or dish. Dissolve bouillon granules in boiling water; mix with taco sauce. Pour mixture over meat. Bake, uncovered, in 350° oven for 1¼ to 1½ hours, basting often. Remove strings. Top meat with green chili strips and cheese. Return to oven to melt cheese, about 5 minutes. Makes 6 servings.

Crockery Cooker Directions: Prepare steak rolls as above. Place in electric slow crockery cooker. Dissolve bouillon granules in boiling water; combine with taco sauce. Pour mixture over meat. Cover; cook at low-heat setting 8 hours. Transfer meat rolls to serving platter; remove strings. Keep meat warm. Pour cooking liquid into saucepan; skim off excess fat. Blend 2 tablespoons *cold water* into 4 teaspoons *cornstarch;* stir into liquid. Cook and stir till mixture is thickened and bubbly. Spoon some sauce over meat; top with chili strips and shredded cheese. Pass remaining sauce.

Rio Grande Pork Roast and Bean-Avocado Salad

Rio Grande Pork Roast

Pictured above

1 4-pound rolled boneless pork loin
   roast
½ cup apple jelly
1 10-ounce can **Old El Paso Mild
   Enchilada Sauce**
   . . .
2 tablespoons cornstarch
2 tablespoons cold water
¼ cup coarsely crushed **Old El Paso
   Taco or Tostada Shells**

Place pork, fat side up, on rack in shallow roasting pan. Roast in 325° oven for 2 to 2½ hours or till meat thermometer registers 165°. In saucepan, bring jelly and enchilada sauce to boiling; reduce heat and simmer, uncovered, for 2 minutes. Blend cornstarch and water; stir into sauce. Cook and stir till thickened and bubbly. Spoon some sauce over roast. Continue roasting till thermometer registers 170°, about 15 minutes more, spooning sauce over occasionally. Remove from oven; let stand 10 minutes. Spoon additional sauce over and sprinkle with crushed taco shells. Garnish with orange slices, if desired. Serve with remaining sauce and *Bean-Avocado Salad* (page 64).

Steak and Vegetable Kabobs

Pictured at right

 1 cup burgundy wine
 1/4 cup cooking oil
 1 envelope **Old El Paso Chili Seasoning Mix** (1/3 cup)
 1/2 teaspoon dried thyme, crushed
 2 pounds beef sirloin steak, cut in 1-inch pieces
 2 zucchini, cut in 1-inch slices
 2 ears corn, cut in 1-inch slices
 2 4-ounce cans **Old El Paso Whole Green Chillies**, seeded and rinsed
 1 envelope **Old El Paso Mexican Rice Seasoning Mix**
 1 cup long-grain rice

In bowl, combine burgundy, oil, chili seasoning mix, and thyme. Add meat pieces and stir to coat well. Cover and marinate at room temperature for 2 hours or overnight in refrigerator. Drain meat, reserving marinade. Salt vegetables. On six skewers, thread meat pieces alternately with slices of zucchini, peppers and corn. Broil kabobs 4 to 6 inches from heat for 4 minutes. Make a quarter turn and brush with additional marinade; broil 4 minutes more. Repeat turning and brushing 2 more times till all sides of meat are browned.

Meanwhile prepare Mexican rice mix and rice according to package directions on mix. Serve kabobs atop Mexican rice.

Stroganoff Pot Roast, Southwestern-Style

 3 to 3 1/2-pound round-bone pot roast
 2 teaspoons seasoned salt
 1 1/2 teaspoons paprika
 1/2 teaspoon cumin
 1/2 teaspoon dried oregano, crushed

· · ·

 2 tablespoons bacon drippings or cooking oil
 1 10-ounce can **Old El Paso Tomatoes and Green Chilies**
 1 teaspoon instant beef bouillon granules
 1/2 cup boiling water
 1 bay leaf

· · ·

 1 to 2 tablespoons all-purpose flour
 1 cup dairy sour cream
 Hot cooked noodles

Trim excess fat from roast. Combine seasoned salt, paprika, cumin, and oregano; rub half over one side of the meat. Pierce with a two-tined fork. Repeat with other side of the meat.

In 5-quart Dutch oven, brown meat on both sides in hot bacon drippings or cooking oil. Add tomatoes and green chilies, bouillon granules dissolved in boiling water, and bay leaf. Cover and simmer 2 hours or till meat is tender. Remove meat to platter; keep warm. Skim fat from pan juices; measure 1 1/2 cups pan juices. Stir flour into sour cream. Return pan juices to Dutch oven; add sour cream mixture. Heat through but do not boil. Serve meat atop noodles; spoon sour cream mixture over all. Makes 6 to 8 servings.

A Mexican Dinner to Everyone's Liking. Pep up the ordinary run-of-the-grill steaks and hamburgers with South-of-the-border flair. Let everyone at the gathering grill the meat just the way he likes it. Offer large strips of seeded **Old El Paso Whole Green Chilies** or, for the braver, strips of **Old El Paso Pickled Chilies Jalapeños** to spread atop the meat. Top them off with slices of Monterey Jack or cheddar cheese. Return to the grill just to heat the chilies and melt the cheese.

Mexican-Up Outdoor Cooking

Durango-Sauced Ribs

Picante sauce means "hot," partner.

2 pounds pork spareribs or loin
    back ribs
    Water
1 8-ounce jar **Old El Paso Mild Taco
    Sauce**
½ small onion, cut up
¼ cup catsup
1 tablespoon brown sugar
1 tablespoon butter or margarine
1 teaspoon **Old El Paso Picante
    Sauce** (optional)
¼ teaspoon paprika
1 thin lemon slice

Cut pork spareribs into 2 pieces. Simmer, covered, in salted water to cover till tender, 40 to 45 minutes; drain.

    Meanwhile, prepare *Barbecue Sauce:* In blender container, blend taco sauce and onion till almost smooth. In saucepan, combine taco sauce mixture, catsup, brown sugar, butter or margarine, picante sauce, paprika, and lemon slice. Bring to boiling; simmer 5 to 8 minutes, till slightly thickened.

    Grill hot ribs over medium to low coals 10 to 15 minutes on each side, brushing often with *Barbecue Sauce.* Pass remaining sauce with ribs. Makes 2 servings.

    Oven Method: Prepare *Barbecue Sauce* and simmer ribs as above. Place ribs in shallow roasting pan; spoon some *Barbecue Sauce* over. Bake in 350° oven for 20 minutes; spoon sauce over occasionally.

Taco-Seasoned Round Steak

Just before removing from grill, top steak with **Old El Paso Whole Green Chilies** or **Hot Pickled Jalapeño Strips** and slices of Monterey Jack cheese, if desired.

1 envelope **Old El Paso Taco
    Seasoning Mix** (⅓ cup)
1 cup water
¼ cup tequila or dry sherry
1 3-pound round steak, cut 1½ to 2
    inches thick

Combine seasoning mix, water, and tequila. Trim excess fat from round steak; slash the fat edge at 1-inch intervals. Place meat in large plastic bag in deep bowl. Pour taco marinade into bag. Seal and marinate several hours or overnight in refrigerator, turning once. Drain, reserving marinade.

    Grill steak over medium coals 3 inches from heat for a total of 30 to 35 minutes for rare doneness, turning steak with tongs frequently and basting with reserved marinade each time. Slice across the grain to serve. Makes 5 or 6 servings.

Some Handy-Dandy Barbecue Tips

—To avoid flare-ups when grilling large pieces of meat, use a drip pan to catch the meat juices. Arange the coals around the pan.

• Use a meat thermometer in roasts as an indicator of doneness. Be sure the tip doesn't touch fat, bone, or the metal spit rod. When the thermometer reaches the desired temperature, push it in a little farther to be sure the meat is done throughout.

• Use tongs to turn the meat. A fork piercing the steak will let juices escape.

• For foods that need frequent turning, like hamburgers and hot dogs or awkward meats such as whole fish and meat loaf, a wire grill basket will help cook your meats to a turn.

• Test the temperature of the coals before starting. Hold your hand palm-side down at the level the food will be cooking. Begin counting "one thousand one, one thousand two;" if you need to withdraw your hand after two seconds the coals are hot, three seconds for medium-hot coals, four seconds for medium coals, and five or six seconds for slow coals.

Durango-Sauced Ribs

Sauced Nachos

Serve these while waiting for the coals to near readiness.

1 medium onion, chopped
2 tablespoons cooking oil
1 10-ounce can **Old El Paso Tomatoes and Green Chilies**
1 teaspoon dried oregano, crushed
6 **Old El Paso Tostada Shells**
24 to 36 1x1x$\frac{1}{4}$-inch pieces Monterey Jack or longhorn cheese
$\frac{1}{4}$ to $\frac{1}{2}$ cup dairy sour cream
Old El Paso Pickled Chilies Jalapeños, seeded, rinsed, and cut in strips (optional)

In medium saucepan, cook onion in the 2 tablespoons oil till tender but not brown. Stir in tomatoes and green chilies and the oregano. Simmer, uncovered, 15 to 20 minutes till very thick.

Break tostada shells in quarters or sixths. Place on baking sheet. Place about 1 teaspoon tomato mixture atop each. Top with a square of cheese, then a dollop of sour cream. Bake in 400° oven for 4 to 5 minutes or till cheese just begins to melt. Garnish top of each with a strip of jalapeño, if desired. Makes 24 to 36 nachos.

Texas Bean Barbecue

A zesty addition to any barbecue lineup.

8 slices bacon, chopped
1 cup chopped onion
2 16-ounce cans yellow hominy, drained
2 15-ounce cans **Old El Paso Mexe-Beans**
1 10-ounce can **Old El Paso Tomatoes and Green Chilies**
2 tablespoons vinegar
1 tablespoon **Old El Paso Jalapeño Relish** (optional)
1 teaspoon salt
2 teaspoons prepared mustard

Cook bacon till almost crisp; drain, reserving 2 tablespoons drippings. Cook onion in reserved drippings till tender but not brown. Combine onion, bacon, drained hominy, Mexe-beans, tomatoes and green chilies, vinegar, jalapeño relish, salt, and mustard. Turn into 2$\frac{1}{2}$-quart casserole. Bake, covered, in 350° oven for 1$\frac{1}{2}$ hours. Makes 10 servings.

Zesty Fiesta Corn

Team with a barbecued turkey or steaks

$\frac{1}{2}$ envelope (about 2 tablespoons) **Old El Paso Taco Seasoning Mix**
$\frac{1}{4}$ cup water
$\frac{1}{4}$ cup salad oil
$\frac{1}{4}$ cup vinegar
1 16-ounce can whole kernel corn, drained
2 medium tomatoes, peeled and diced (about 1$\frac{1}{2}$ cups)
$\frac{1}{2}$ cup sliced pitted ripe olives
$\frac{1}{4}$ cup **Old El Paso Chopped Green Chilies**

In large bowl, combine taco seasoning mix and water; add salad oil and vinegar. Add corn, diced tomatoes, olives, and chilies; toss lightly. Chill mixture several hours or overnight; stir occasionally. Makes 6 servings.

Texas-Style Cornish Hens

4 frozen Rock Cornish game hens
   (12 to 16 ounces each)
  Salt
  Pepper

. . .

¹/₄ cup finely chopped onion
1 clove garlic, minced
2 tablespoons butter or margarine
2 tablespoons brown sugar
2 teaspoons dry mustard
1 10-ounce can **Old El Paso Mild
  Enchilada Sauce**
2 lemon slices, quartered

Season cavity of each bird with a little salt and pepper. Skewer neck and tail openings closed. Run spit through each bird below breastbone and secure with holding forks. Space birds about 1 inch apart on rod. With four 36-inch pieces of cord, tie tail to crossed legs. Bring cord around to back, cross, and bring around and across breast, securing wings to body. Tie knot; cut off loose ends. Place the spit on rotisserie 6 inches over hot coals and turn on motor. Roast birds till leg joints move easily, about 45 minutes.

Meanwhile, prepare *Texas Sauce:* In saucepan, cook onion and garlic in butter or margarine till onion is tender but not brown. Stir in brown sugar and dry mustard till smooth; stir in enchilada sauce and lemon slices. Simmer 15 minutes. Roast birds 10 to 15 minutes more, basting with sauce mixture. Pass extra sauce. Makes 4 servings.

Oven Roasting Method: Prepare *Texas Sauce* as above. Place birds, breast side up, on rack in shallow roasting pan. Cover loosely with foil and roast for 30 minutes.

Uncover and roast 1 hour more or till drumstick moves up and down and twists easily in socket. Baste with *Texas Sauce* last 15 minutes.

Easy-Going Dinners or Buffets

Mexican-Style Chicken

Pictured at right

1   2½- to 3-pound broiler-fryer
      chicken, cut up
      Salt
      Pepper
3   tablespoons cooking oil
            · · ·
½   cup chopped onion
1   cup tomato juice
2   cups chicken broth
            · · ·
1   envelope **Old El Paso Mexican
      Rice Seasoning Mix**
¾   cup regular long-grain rice
1   10-ounce package frozen peas,
      broken apart (2 cups)

Season chicken with a little salt and pepper. In large skillet, brown chicken in hot oil; drain. Add onion, tomato juice, and ½ *cup* of the chicken broth. Cover; simmer 20 minutes. Add seasoning mix, rice, and remaining broth. Return to boiling. Reduce heat; cover and simmer 20 minutes. Add peas; cover and simmer 5 minutes more or till peas are tender, stirring once or twice. Makes 4 servings.

Mexican Chef's Salad

Cheese sauce may be made ahead and served cold. Increase milk in sauce to 1 cup. Chill till serving time.

6   cups torn lettuce
2   carrots, shredded
2   stalks celery, diced
            · · ·
1   cup cooked ham cut in julienne
      strips
1   cup cooked chicken cut in
      julienne strips
2   tomatoes, peeled, cored, and
      diced
3   tablespoons sliced green onion
      with tops
            · · ·
2   cups (8 ounces) shredded sharp
      American cheese
⅔   cup milk
½   can **Old El Paso Whole Green
      Chilies**, seeded, rinsed, and
      chopped
3   tablespoons sliced, pitted ripe
      olives
            · · ·
2   cups coarsely crushed **Old El
      Paso Taco or Tostada Shells**
      Old El Paso Taco Sauce

In large salad bowl, combine lettuce, carrot, and celery. Arrange ham, chicken, tomatoes, and green onion atop. In heavy saucepan, combine cheese and milk. Cook and stir over low heat till cheese is melted and mixture is smooth. Stir in chilies and olives.

Just before serving, pour sauce over salad. Toss lightly. Serve at once. Pass crushed taco shells and taco sauce to sprinkle atop. Makes 6 servings.

El Paso Bean Bake

½ cup chopped onion
1 clove garlic, minced
6 tablespoons cooking oil
4 teaspoons all-purpose flour
2 15-ounce cans **Old El Paso Mexe-Beans**
1 7½-ounce can **Old El Paso Tomatoes and Jalapeños**

· · ·

⅔ cup yellow cornmeal
¾ teaspoon salt
¼ teaspoon baking soda
1 beaten egg
½ cup milk
1 12-ounce can whole kernel corn with sweet peppers, drained
1 cup (4 ounces) shredded American cheese

In large saucepan, cook onion and garlic in *2 table-spoons* of the oil till onion is tender but not brown. Blend in flour. Stir in Mexe-beans and tomatoes and jalapeños. Cook and stir till slightly thickened and bubbly. Remove from heat; set aside.

In bowl, combine cornmeal, salt, and soda. Combine egg, milk, and the remaining 4 tablespoons cooking oil. Add to dry ingredients along with the corn; mix well. (Mixture will be thin.) Pour about ⅔ of the cornmeal mixture into greased 2-quart casserole or a 12x7½x2-inch baking dish. Sprinkle with cheese; spoon bean mixture over all. Spoon remaining cornmeal mixture around edge of casserole. Bake, uncovered, in 350° oven 35 minutes or till cornmeal topper is done. Makes 8 to 10 servings.

Tostada Pizza

2 tablespoons yellow cornmeal
2 cups packaged biscuit mix
½ cup water

· · ·

1 pound ground beef
3 tablespoons **Old El Paso Chopped Green Chilies**
1 envelope **Old El Paso Taco Seasoning Mix** (⅓ cup)
¾ cup water

· · ·

1 16-ounce can **Old El Paso Refried Beans**
1 cup (4 ounces) shredded sharp American cheese
1 cup shredded lettuce
1 tomato, chopped
½ cup chopped onion
Old El Paso Taco Sauce

Sprinkle a well-greased 12-inch pizza pan with cornmeal. Combine biscuit mix and the ½ cup water. Stir with fork till dough follows fork around bowl. Turn dough out on lightly floured surface; knead 5 or 6 times. Roll to 14-inch circle; pat into prepared pizza pan, crimping edges. Bake in 425° oven 12 minutes or till golden brown.

Meanwhile, in skillet, brown meat; drain off excess fat. Stir in chilies, taco seasoning mix, and the ¾ cup water; bring to boiling. Reduce heat; simmer, uncovered, 10 to 15 minutes.

Spread refried beans over crust; top with meat mixture. Bake in 425° oven for 8 to 10 minutes. Top with cheese; bake 2 minutes more. Pass lettuce, tomato, onion, and taco sauce to sprinkle over top. Makes 6 servings.

Spread out an appetizer buffet. Check out the Sundown Appetizer section, pages 46 through 51, and the Mariachi Dip and Nibbles chapter, pages 52 through 55. Many of the delectables can be made ahead to chill before serving or prepared ahead to heat at the last minute. To simplify the beverage selections, offer a chilly pitcher of Sangria or a choice of red or white wine.

Meaty Roll-Ups

Perfect for a buffet—

8 ounces finely diced uncooked
   pork
8 ounces finely diced uncooked
   beef
1 tablespoon cooking oil
2 tablespoons all-purpose flour
1/2 teaspoon salt
   Dash pepper
1 16-ounce can tomatoes, cut up
1/2 cup chopped onion
2 **Old El Paso Pickled Chilies**
   Jalapeños, seeded, rinsed, and
   chopped
1 small clove garlic, minced
12 **Old El Paso Tortillas**

In medium skillet, cook pork and beef in hot oil till browned. Drain off excess fat. Stir in flour, salt, and pepper. Add undrained tomatoes, onion, peppers, and garlic. Cook and stir over medium heat till thickened and bubbly.

Place tortillas on baking sheet. Heat in warm oven for 4 to 5 minutes. Spoon about 1/4 cup meat filling in center of each tortilla; roll up. Makes 12 roll-ups.

Chicken and Sausage Tostadas

2 tablespoons salad oil
1 tablespoon lemon juice
1/4 teaspoon dried oregano, crushed
1/8 teaspoon salt
   Dash pepper
2 onion slices, separated into rings
   . . .
2 cups cooked chicken cut in strips
   Water
   . . .
1 pound bulk pork sausage
1/2 cup chopped onion
1 clove garlic, minced
1 16-ounce can **Old El Paso Refried**
   Beans
1 10-ounce can **Old El Paso Hot**
   Enchilada Sauce
   . . .
10 **Old El Paso Tostada Shells**
4 cups chopped lettuce

In small bowl, combine the 2 tablespoons salad oil, the lemon juice, oregano, salt, and pepper; add the onion rings. Cover; marinate in refrigerator at least 2 hours.

In saucepan, combine chicken and a few tablespoons water. Heat through; keep warm over low heat.

In skillet, combine sausage, the chopped onion, and garlic; cook till meat is browned. Drain off excess fat. Add refried beans and enchilada sauce. Cook, stirring frequently, till mixture is heated through.

Spread each tostada with bean mixture. Drain onion rings, reserving marinade. Toss lettuce with reserved marinade; spoon atop beans. Top with the hot chicken strips and marinated onion rings. Makes 10 tostadas.

Share the load. Have the gang over, but give them a recipe from the following menu to prepare and bring along.

Guacamole (recipe page 10) served with **Old El Paso Tostada Shells,** quartered

Chicken Enchiladas (recipe page 82)
3-Bean Salad (recipe page 40)
Taco Biscuits (recipe page 60)
Fresh fruit and selection of cheese
Coffee or white wine

Marinated Shrimp in Avocado Halves

This elegant first course or luncheon entree is pictured at right in back.

12 ounces fresh or frozen shelled
    medium shrimp
2 tablespoons vinegar
1½ teaspoons lemon juice
¼ teaspoon salt
⅛ teaspoon dry mustard
    Dash pepper
      . . .
1 small onion, thinly sliced
1 clove garlic, halved
3 tablespoons cooking oil
1 **Old El Paso Pickled Chilies**
    Jalapeños, seeded, rinsed, and
    cut in strips
      . . .
2 avocados, halved and seeded
1 medium tomato, chopped

Thaw frozen shrimp. In bowl, combine vinegar, lemon juice, salt, mustard, and pepper; set aside.

In medium skillet, cook shrimp, *half* the onion slices, and the garlic in hot oil over medium-high heat 4 to 5 minutes or just till shrimp are done, stirring occasionally. Remove onion and garlic with slotted spoon; discard. Add shrimp and the remaining oil from skillet to vinegar mixture in bowl along with remaining sliced onion and the jalapeño. Cover and chill several hours or overnight, stirring occasionally.

To serve, lift shrimp, onion slices, and jalapeño from marinade; spoon into avocado halves. Sprinkle with chopped tomato; drizzle some of the marinade over all. Makes 4 servings.

Shrimp-Avocado Tostadas

1 cup Guacamole (recipe page 10)
¼ cup sliced green onion
1 tablespoon lemon juice
¼ teaspoon garlic salt
2 4½-ounce cans shrimp, drained
      . . .
8 **Old El Paso Tostada Shells**
3 cups shredded lettuce
2 medium tomatoes, chopped
1 cup (4 ounces) shredded cheddar
    cheese

In small bowl, combine Guacamole, green onion, lemon juice, and garlic salt; stir in shrimp. Warm tostada shells according to the package directions.

To assemble tostadas, spoon some of the shredded lettuce and chopped tomato onto each warm tostada shell. Top each with some of the shrimp-avocado mixture. Sprinkle with shredded cheddar cheese. Makes 8 tostadas.

Shrimp Fritters

1 medium onion, finely chopped
1 clove garlic, minced
2 tablespoons cooking oil
1 10-ounce can **Old El Paso**
    Tomatoes and Green Chilies
¾ teaspoon salt
    Dash pepper
      . . .
2 cups packaged biscuit mix
½ cup cold water
1 slightly beaten egg
2 4½-ounce cans shrimp, drained
    and coarsely chopped
      . . .
    Fat for frying

In saucepan, cook onion and garlic in hot oil till onion is tender but not brown. Stir in tomatoes and green chilies, ½ *teaspoon* of the salt, and the pepper. Bring to boiling; reduce heat. Simmer, uncovered, 20 minutes. Cover and keep warm.

Stir together biscuit mix, water, the remaining ¼ teaspoon salt, and the egg till smooth. Fold in shrimp. In deep skillet or saucepan, heat 1 inch fat to 365°. Spoon shrimp mixture into the hot fat (use 1 tablespoon shrimp mixture for small fritter or 2 tablespoons for large one). Fry about 1 minute on each side for small fritters and 2 minutes for large. Drain on paper toweling. Serve hot with the tomato mixture. Makes 20 small or 10 large fritters.

Marinated Shrimp in Avocado Halves and Rice with Crab

Rice with Crab

This peppy main dish is pictured above in foreground.

1 cup long-grain rice
1 small onion, chopped (¼ cup)
2 tablespoons cooking oil

・ ・ ・

3 cups water
¼ cup **Old El Paso Jalapeño Relish**
1 envelope **Old El Paso Mexican Rice Seasoning Mix**

・ ・ ・

½ cup frozen peas
1 7- or 7¼-ounce can crabmeat, drained, broken in chunks, and cartilage removed *or* 7-ounce package frozen shelled shrimp, cooked
1 large tomato, peeled, cored, and coarsely chopped

In skillet, cook rice and onion in hot oil over medium-low heat, stirring frequently, till rice is golden brown, 7 to 10 minutes. Remove from heat.

Stir in water, jalapeño relish, and Mexican rice seasoning mix. Cover and simmer 20 minutes or till most of the liquid is absorbed. Stir in peas; cook 5 minutes more. Gently stir in crab or shrimp and tomato; heat through, 1 to 2 minutes more. Makes 5 servings.

Entertaining Inexpensively

West Texas-Style Hot Chili

Sprinkle shredded cheese and crushed **Old El Paso Taco Shells** over the top, if you like.

  5 slices bacon
  8 ounces Italian sausage links,
    sliced
1¹/₂ pounds beef stew meat, diced
  2 medium onions, chopped (1 cup)
  1 clove garlic, minced
    · · ·
  1 4-ounce can **Old El Paso Whole
    Green Chilies**, seeded, rinsed,
    and chopped
  2 **Old El Paso Pickled Chilies
    Jalapeños,** seeded, rinsed, and
    chopped
  1 to 1¹/₂ tablespoons chili powder
¹/₂ teaspoon salt
¹/₄ teaspoon dried oregano, crushed
2¹/₂ cups water
  1 12-ounce can tomato paste
    · · ·
  1 15-ounce can **Old El Paso
    Mexe-Beans**

In large saucepan or Dutch oven, cook bacon till crisp; drain and crumble. Discard drippings; set bacon aside. Brown sausage in same pan. Drain sausage, reserving 2 tablespoons drippings; set sausage aside. In reserved drippings, brown diced beef, onions, and garlic. Add the cooked sausage, green chilies, jalapeños, chili powder, salt, and oregano. Stir in water and tomato paste. Bring to boiling; simmer, uncovered, for 1¹/₂ hours, stirring occasionally. Stir in beans; simmer, covered, 30 minutes more. Makes 8 servings.

Microwave Directions: In 3-quart glass casserole, layer bacon and paper towels. Micro-cook on high power for 4¹/₂ to 5 minutes. Crumble bacon; set aside. Micro-cook sausage in same casserole on high power for 5 minutes, stirring 3 times; drain off fat.

Stir in beef, onion, garlic, bacon, chilies, jalapeños, chili powder, salt, oregano, *2 cups* water, and tomato paste. Micro-cook, covered, on medium power for 45 minutes. Stir in beans. Micro-cook, covered, on medium power for 30 to 35 minutes.

Acapulco Bean Casserole

An easy casserole off the pantry shelf—and it only takes a nibble out of your food budget.

  1 cup chopped onion
  1 cup chopped celery
  2 tablespoons butter or margarine
  2 15-ounce cans **Old El Paso Chili
    with Beans**
  1 16-ounce can **Old El Paso Refried
    Beans**
  1 12-ounce can whole kernel corn,
    drained
  1 8-ounce jar **Old El Paso Mild** or
    Hot Taco Sauce
¹/₄ teaspoon salt
 10 **Old El Paso Tortillas,** torn
  1 cup (4 ounces) shredded sharp
    cheddar cheese

In saucepan, cook onion and celery in butter or margarine till tender but not brown, about 10 minutes. Stir in chili with beans, refried beans, corn, taco sauce, and salt. Arrange *half* the tortilla pieces in bottom of 13x9x2-inch baking dish; top with *half* the chili mixture; repeat layers.

Bake, covered, in 350° oven for 45 to 50 minutes. Sprinkle cheese atop; return to oven to melt cheese, 2 to 3 minutes. Makes 8 servings.

Mexican Stack-Ups

1 pound ground beef
1/2 cup chopped onion
1 11-ounce can condensed cheddar
  cheese soup
1 11¼-ounce can condensed chili
  beef soup
1 envelope **Old El Paso Enchilada
  Sauce Mix**
1 soup can (1⅓ cups) water
· · ·
18 **Old El Paso Tortillas**
3 slices sharp American cheese

In small skillet, cook ground beef and onion till meat is brown and onion is tender; drain off excess fat. Stir in cheddar cheese soup, chili beef soup, enchilada sauce mix, and water. Heat mixture to boiling; reduce heat and simmer about 5 minutes, stirring frequently.

Place 6 tortillas in bottom of 13x9x2-inch baking pan. Top each with ⅓ the meat mixture. Place 6 more tortillas over. Top with another ⅓ of the meat. Repeat layers ending with meat. Bake in 350° oven for 15 minutes or till mixture is heated through.

Cut cheese slices diagonally into quarters. Place 2 quarters atop each tortilla stack. Return to oven to melt cheese, 2 to 3 minutes more. Makes 6 servings.

Mexican Cheese Fondue

For a more Mexican flavor, substitute broken tostada shell dippers for the French bread.

1 17-ounce can cream-style corn
1 15-ounce can tomato sauce with
  tomato tidbits
1 4-ounce can **Old El Paso Whole
  Green Chilies,** seeded, rinsed,
  and chopped
1 teaspoon chili powder
4 cups (16 ounces) shredded sharp
  American cheese
· · ·
2 tablespoons cold water
2 tablespoons cornstarch
  French bread, cut in bite-size
  cubes, each with crust

Crockery Cooker Directions: In crockery cooker, combine corn, tomato sauce, chili peppers, and chili powder; add cheese. Cover; cook on high-heat setting till cheese is melted, about 1 hour, stirring occasionally. Blend cold water slowly into cornstarch; stir into cheese mixture. Cook on high-heat setting till thickened, about 10 minutes more, stirring often. Serve at once or reduce heat and keep warm, covered, on low-heat setting for 1 to 2 hours; stir occasionally. Spear bread cube with fondue fork; dip in fondue, swirling to coat. Makes 10 to 12 servings.

Set the Mexican Mood. The fiesta atmosphere puts the guests immediately at ease, while an easy-on-the-budget menu makes the dinner a festive occasion for the hostess, too.

Start with a bright tablecloth and top with brightly colored streamers of crepe paper for runners. Accent festive napkins with crepe paper flower napkin rings.

The centerpiece might be an explosion of brightly colored crepe paper flowers or a homemade piñata of papier-maché.

Rio Grande Stew

Pictured at right

2 pounds boneless beef for stew, cut in 1½-inch cubes
2 tablespoons cooking oil
3 cups water
1 10-ounce can condensed beef broth
½ cup chopped celery
½ cup chopped onion
2 cloves garlic, minced
1 envelope **Old El Paso Chili Seasoning Mix** (⅓ cup)
2 bay leaves
1½ teaspoons salt
2 tablespoons cold water
2 tablespoons cornstarch
3 medium carrots, cut in chunks
2 ears fresh corn on the cob, cut in 1-inch pieces
1 15-ounce can **Old El Paso Garbanzos**
8 cabbage wedges
1 16-ounce can tomatoes, cut up
½ cup finely chopped onion
1 4-ounce can **Old El Paso Whole Green Chilies**, seeded, rinsed, and chopped
1 clove garlic, minced
¼ cup snipped parsley
½ teaspoon salt

In large Dutch oven, brown half the beef at a time in hot oil; return all meat to pan. Add the 3 cups water, the beef broth, the celery, the ½ cup chopped onion, the 2 cloves garlic, the chili seasoning mix, bay leaves and the 1½ teaspoons salt. Bring to boiling; reduce heat. Cover and simmer till meat is almost tender, about 2 hours.

Skim off fat from top of stew. Blend together the cold water and the cornstarch; stir into stew. Cook and stir till bubbly. Add carrot, corn, and undrained garbanzos; arrange cabbage atop. Simmer, covered, 20 to 30 minutes, or till meat and vegetables are done.

Remove and discard bay leaves. Season to taste with additional salt and pepper. Serve stew in bowls; pass *Salsa* to spoon over each serving. Makes 8 servings.

To make *Salsa:* Combine undrained tomatoes, the finely chopped onion, the chilies, the remaining garlic, the parsley, and the remaining ½ teaspoon salt.

Taco Peppers

6 green bell peppers
1 14½-ounce can **Old El Paso Tamales**
1 15-ounce can **Old El Paso Chili with Beans**
1 cup (4 ounces) shredded sharp cheddar cheese
¼ cup catsup
¼ cup chopped onion
1½ cups coarsely crushed **Old El Paso Taco or Tostada Shells**

Electric Skillet Directions: Cut peppers in half lengthwise; remove stems, seeds, and membrane. Cook peppers in a large amount of boiling, salted water for 5 minutes. Drain and salt insides lightly. Drain tamales and remove wrappers; slice tamales in ½-inch pieces. Combine chili, ½ *cup* of the cheese, the catsup, and onion; fold in tamale pieces. Fill peppers with chili mixture.

Place peppers in electric skillet; pour hot water around peppers to depth of ¼ inch. Cover and simmer with vent open for 25 minutes or till filling is heated through and peppers are tender. Top peppers with remaining cheese; sprinkle with crushed taco shells. Heat, uncovered, till cheese melts, 1 to 2 minutes more. Makes 6 servings.

Enchiladas of All Sorts

Chicken Enchiladas

- 2 large chicken breasts
  Water
  Salt
- 1 cup chopped onion
- 1 clove garlic, minced
- 2 tablespoons butter or margarine
- 1 16-ounce can tomatoes, cut up
- 1 8-ounce can tomato sauce
- 1 4-ounce can **Old El Paso Whole Green Chilies**, seeded, rinsed, and chopped
- 1 teaspoon sugar
- 1 teaspoon ground cumin
- 1/2 teaspoon salt
- 1/2 teaspoon dried oregano, crushed
- 1/2 teaspoon dried basil, crushed
- 12 **Old El Paso Tortillas**
- 2 1/2 cups (10 ounces) shredded Monterey Jack cheese
- 3/4 cup dairy sour cream

In saucepan, simmer chicken breasts in water to cover, 15 to 20 minutes or till tender. Drain and carefully remove skin and bones. Sprinkle chicken with a little salt. Cut in 12 strips; set aside.

In saucepan, cook onion and garlic in butter or margarine till tender but not brown. Add tomatoes, tomato sauce, chilies, sugar, cumin, the 1/2 teaspoon salt, the oregano, and basil. Bring to boiling; reduce heat. Dip each tortilla in tomato mixture to soften. Place one piece of chicken and about 2 tablespoons shredded cheese on each tortilla; roll up and place, seam side down, in 13x9x2-inch baking dish. Blend sour cream into remaining sauce mixture; pour over tortillas. Sprinkle with remaining cheese. Cover and bake in 350° oven for 40 minutes or till heated through. Makes 6 servings.

Enchilada Casserole

- 1 1/2 pounds ground beef
- 1/2 cup chopped onion
- 1 16-ounce can **Old El Paso Refried Beans**
- 1/2 teaspoon salt
- 1/4 teaspoon pepper
- 3 tablespoons cooking oil
- 12 **Old El Paso Tortillas**
- 2 tomatoes, peeled and chopped
- 1/4 cup butter or margarine
- 1/4 cup all-purpose flour
- 1/2 teaspoon salt
- 1/4 teaspoon paprika
- 2 cups milk
- 1 10-ounce can **Old El Paso Mild Enchilada Sauce**
- 1 1/2 cups (6 ounces) shredded cheddar cheese
- 3/4 cup sliced ripe olives

In skillet, cook beef and onion till meat is brown and onion is tender; drain. Stir in beans, the first 1/2 teaspoon salt, and the pepper.

In another skillet, heat oil. Quickly dip tortillas in hot oil just till softened. Place 1/3 cup meat mixture on each tortilla. Top each with chopped tomato; roll tightly. Place, seam side down, in 13x9x2-inch baking dish. Melt butter or margarine; stir in flour, the remaining 1/2 teaspoon salt, and the paprika. Add milk and enchilada sauce. Cook and stir till boiling; boil 1 minute. Stir in cheese and olives; pour over tortillas. Bake in 350° oven for 30 minutes. Makes 6 servings.

Hot Pepper Enchiladas

Peppy Jalapeño Relish is the key flavor maker.

3 tablespoons cooking oil
12 **Old El Paso Tortillas**
2 cups (8 ounces) shredded
   Monterey Jack cheese
3/4 cup finely chopped onion
2 tablespoons butter or margarine
3 tablespoons all-purpose flour
1 1/3 cups chicken broth
1/4 cup **Old El Paso Jalapeño Relish**
1/2 cup dairy sour cream
1/4 teaspoon salt

In small skillet, heat oil. Dip each tortilla in hot oil for 5 seconds per side, or just till limp. Drain on paper toweling. Place 2 tablespoons of the shredded cheese and 1 tablespoon onion on each tortilla; roll up. Place tortillas, seam side down, in 12x7 1/2x2-inch baking dish.

In medium saucepan, melt butter or margarine; blend in flour. Add chicken broth all at once; cook, stirring constantly, till mixture thickens and bubbles. Stir 1/4 cup of the relish, the sour cream, and the salt into the sauce; cook till heated through, but do not boil. Pour sauce over rolled tortillas in baking dish. Bake in 400° oven for 18 to 20 minutes. Sprinkle the remaining 1/2 cup shredded cheese atop tortillas; return to oven to melt cheese, 2 to 3 minutes. Pass additional **Old El Paso Jalapeño Relish** to spoon atop enchiladas, if desired. Makes 6 servings.

Cottage Enchiladas

1 4-ounce can **Old El Paso Whole
   Green Chilies**
12 **Old El Paso Tortillas**
   Cooking oil
1 cup dairy sour cream
1 12-ounce carton (1 1/2 cups)
   cream-style cottage cheese
1/2 teaspoon salt
   Dash pepper
8 ounces sharp American cheese,
   cut in 12 strips
1 14-ounce can **Old El Paso Mild
   Enchilada Sauce**

Drain chilies; remove seeds and rinse. Cut chilies in 12 strips. Dip tortillas in hot oil till limp, about 5 seconds on each side; drain on paper toweling.

Combine sour cream, cottage cheese, salt, and pepper. Reserve 1/2 cup of the mixture; spoon remaining mixture onto tortillas. Top each with a strip of green chili and a strip of cheese; roll up. Place, seam-side down, in 12x7 1/2x2-inch baking dish.

Combine reserved sour cream mixture and enchilada sauce; pour over tortillas. Bake in 350° oven for 25 to 30 minutes. Garnish with ripe olive slices, if desired. Makes 6 servings.

Enchiladas—the meal makers.

Depending on the recipe, enchiladas can be easy or involved but they all have a substantial great taste in common. There are other pluses, too.

• Tortillas and sauce deliciously stretch any meat into a family-pleasing meal.

• Easy enchilada casseroles boast convenience—they can be made ahead, covered, and refrigerated till time to bake.

• Enchiladas dress up leftover meat to make on-hands into a delightful dinner.

• Cheese-filled enchiladas make a lenten dinner a treat.

Enchilada Squares

1 pound ground beef
¼ cup chopped onion

. . .

4 eggs
1 8-ounce can tomato sauce
1 5⅓-ounce can Pet evaporated milk
1 envelope **Old El Paso Enchilada Sauce Mix**
⅓ cup sliced pitted ripe olives
2 cups coarsely crushed **Old El Paso Taco or Tostada Shells**
1 cup (4 ounces) shredded cheddar cheese

In skillet, cook beef and onion till meat is brown and onion is tender. Drain off excess fat. Spread meat mixture in 10x6x2-inch baking dish.

Beat together eggs, tomato sauce, evaporated milk, and enchilada sauce mix; pour over meat. Sprinkle with olives; top with taco or tostada shells. Bake, uncovered, in 350° oven 20 to 25 minutes or till knife inserted just off center comes out clean. Sprinkle with cheese. Return to oven to melt cheese, 2 to 3 minutes. Makes 6 servings.

Enchilada Dos

½ pound lean ground beef
¼ cup chopped onion
¼ teaspoon salt
4 **Old El Paso Tortillas**
¼ cup **Old El Paso Taco Sauce**
½ cup (2 ounces) shredded Monterey Jack cheese
2 tablespoons butter or margarine
3 tablespoons all-purpose flour
1 teaspoon instant chicken bouillon granules
1 cup water
½ cup dairy sour cream
2 tablespoons **Old El Paso Chopped Green Chilies**

Microwave Directions: In glass bowl, crumble ground beef. Add onion. Micro-cook, uncovered, on high power for 2 minutes, stirring occasionally to break up meat. Drain. Add salt.

Wrap tortillas in paper toweling. Micro-cook 15 seconds or till softened. Divide meat among the 4 tortillas; top each with 1 tablespoon of the taco sauce and 1 tablespoon cheese. Roll up. Place, seam side down, in 9-inch glass pie plate. In 2-cup glass measuring cup, melt butter in microwave for 20 seconds. Blend in flour. Stir in bouillon granules and water.

Cook, uncovered, till mixture thickens and bubbles, 2 minutes, stirring every 30 seconds. Stir moderate amount of hot mixture into sour cream; return all to hot mixture. Stir in chilies. Pour mixture over tortillas. Sprinkle with remaining cheese. Micro-cook on high power 3 minutes or till hot through. Makes 2 servings.

Pork-Stuffed Enchiladas

1½ cups cubed cooked pork
1 cup (4 ounces) shredded Monterey Jack cheese
½ cup chopped onion
1 10¾-ounce can condensed tomato soup
1 10¾-ounce can condensed cream of mushroom soup
1 10-ounce can **Old El Paso Hot Enchilada Sauce**
12 **Old El Paso Tortillas**

Combine meat, ½ *cup* of the cheese, and the onion; set aside. In saucepan, combine soups and enchilada sauce; heat to boiling. Quickly dip tortillas in sauce. Divide meat mixture among tortillas; roll up. Place in 12x7½x2-inch baking dish. Top with remaining sauce and sprinkle with remaining cheese. Bake in 350° oven for 25 to 30 minutes. Makes 6 servings.

Skillet Enchiladas

Skillet Enchiladas

Pictured above

  1 pound ground beef
1/2 cup chopped onion
  1 10³/4-ounce can condensed cream
     of mushroom soup
  1 10-ounce can **Old El Paso Mild
     Enchilada Sauce**
1/3 cup milk
  2 tablespoons **Old El Paso Chopped
     Green Chilies**

    . . .

  8 **Old El Paso Tortillas**
     Cooking oil
2¹/2 cups (10 ounces) shredded sharp
     American cheese
1/2 cup chopped pitted ripe olives

In 10-inch skillet, cook ground beef and onion till meat is brown and onion is tender; drain off excess fat. Stir in soup, enchilada sauce, milk, and chilies. Reduce heat; cover and simmer 20 minutes, stirring occasionally.

In small skillet, dip tortillas in hot oil just till limp, about 5 seconds on each side. Drain on paper toweling. Reserve 1/2 cup cheese; place 1/4 cup of the remaining cheese on each tortilla. Sprinkle with olives. Roll up each tortilla. Place in sauce in skillet; cover and cook till heated through, 5 minutes. Sprinkle with reserved cheese, cover and cook till cheese melts, about 1 minute. Makes 4 servings.

Stacked Enchiladas

¹/₂ cup finely chopped onion
2 tablespoons cooking oil
1 tablespoon all-purpose flour
¹/₂ cup milk
1 4-ounce can **Old El Paso Whole Green Chilies**, seeded, rinsed, and chopped
¹/₂ teaspoon salt

. . .

2 cups diced cooked beef
2 tomatoes, peeled, and chopped

. . .

2 tablespoons cooking oil
8 **Old El Paso Tortillas**
1 cup (4 ounces) shredded Monterey Jack cheese

In skillet, cook onion in 2 tablespoons oil till tender but not brown. Blend in flour. Add milk, chilies, and salt. Cook, stirring constantly, till thickened and bubbly. Stir in beef and tomatoes. Heat through; keep warm.

In small skillet, heat 2 tablespoons oil. Dip tortillas one at a time in the hot oil about 5 seconds on each side or till limp. Drain on paper toweling. Place a hot tortilla in 9x9x2-inch baking pan. Top with about ¹/₄ cup beef mixture and 2 tablespoons of cheese. Layer on remaining tortillas, beef mixture, and cheese to make a stack. Bake in 350° oven for 20 minutes or till hot. Unstack to serve. Makes 4 servings.

Guacamole-Topped Roll-Ups

3 tablespoons butter or margarine
3 tablespoons all-purpose flour
1 teaspoon salt
1 cup chicken broth
1 tablespoon snipped parsley
1 tablespoon lemon juice
1 teaspoon grated onion
1 4-ounce can **Old El Paso Whole Green Chilies**, seeded, rinsed, and chopped
2 cups finely diced cooked chicken
Cooking oil
18 **Old El Paso Tortillas**
Guacamole (recipe page 10)

In saucepan, melt butter or margarine; blend in flour and salt. Add chicken broth. Cook and stir till mixture thickens and bubbles. Add parsley, lemon juice, and onion. Stir in chilies and chicken; cool slightly.

In small skillet, heat cooking oil. Dip tortillas in hot oil 5 seconds on each side till limp. Drain on paper toweling. Divide chicken mixture among tortillas; roll up. Place, seam side down, in 12x7¹/₂x2-inch baking dish. Cover with foil; bake in 350° oven 30 to 35 minutes till heated through. Serve topped with Guacamole. Makes 4 servings.

Super Beefy Enchiladas

1¹/₂ cups cubed cooked beef
1 cup (4 ounces) shredded sharp cheddar cheese
¹/₂ cup chopped onion
1 10³/₄-ounce can condensed cream of mushroom soup
1 10³/₄-ounce can condensed tomato soup
1 10-ounce can **Old El Paso Hot Enchilada Sauce**
12 **Old El Paso Tortillas**

Combine beef, *half* of the cheese, and the chopped onion; set aside. In saucepan, combine soups and the enchilada sauce; bring to boiling. Quickly dip tortillas in sauce. Divide meat mixture among tortillas; roll up. Place in 12x7¹/₂x2-inch baking dish. Top with remaining sauce and the remaining cheese. Bake in 350° oven 25 to 30 minutes. Makes 6 servings.

Fried Enchiladas

To keep the tortillas rolled when dipping them in the batter, you may want to secure them with a wooden pick.

1/2 cup chopped onion
1/4 cup water
1 15-ounce can tomato puree
1 or 2 **Old El Paso Pickled Chilies Jalapeños,** seeded, rinsed, and chopped
1/4 teaspoon salt

. . .

1 pound ground pork
1 cup chopped onion
2 medium potatoes, cooked, peeled, and chopped
1 1/2 teaspoon salt

. . .

4 egg whites
4 egg yolks
1 tablespoon water
2 tablespoons all-purpose flour
1/4 teaspoon salt

. . .

2 tablespoons cooking oil
12 **Old El Paso Tortillas**
Fat for deep-fat frying
Shredded lettuce
Shredded cheddar cheese

In covered saucepan, cook the 1/2 cup onion in the 1/4 cup water about 5 minutes till tender. Stir in 1 1/4 *cups* of the tomato puree, the chopped jalapeños, and the 1/4 teaspoon salt. Heat to boiling; simmer, covered, 10 minutes. Uncover; simmer 2 to 3 minutes more or till slightly thickened. Set aside.

In skillet, cook pork and the 1 cup onion till pork is brown and onion is tender. Drain off excess fat. Stir in remaining 1/2 cup tomato puree, the cooked potatoes, and the 1 1/2 teaspoons salt. Heat through. Set filling aside.

Beat egg whites till stiff peaks form. Beat egg yolks and the 1 tablespoon water slightly. Add flour and the 1/4 teaspoon salt; beat about 3 minutes or till thick and lemon-colored. Fold into whites.

To assemble enchiladas, heat the 2 tablespoons oil in skillet. Dip each tortilla in the hot oil 5 seconds per side or till limp. Spoon about 1/4 cup filling onto each tortilla; roll up. Dip filled tortillas in egg mixture, being sure ends are covered. Cook in deep hot fat (375°) about 2 minutes per side or till golden brown. Drain on paper toweling. Reheat sauce. Arrange enchiladas on a platter; pour sauce over. Garnish with lettuce and cheese. Makes 6 servings.

Rolling 'em up. There are a few ways to get an **Old El Paso Tortilla** to roll over for enchiladas—

• In a 6-inch skillet, heat about 2 tablespoons cooking oil over medium heat. Holding tortilla with tongs, dip each tortilla in the hot oil for 5 seconds per side or till tortilla is limp. The tortilla will become too crisp to roll if held in oil too long.

Drain limp tortillas on paper toweling. Repeat with remaining tortillas, adding more oil as needed.

• For a microwave, wrap the tortillas in paper toweling. Micro-cook on high power 15 to 30 seconds or till tortillas are warm and softened.

• Wrap tortillas tightly in foil. Heat in 350° oven for 10 to 20 minutes or till heated through.

• If you have a sauce you've made for the recipe, dip the tortilla in the hot sauce till it's limp.

Creamy Chicken Enchiladas

Garnish with **Old El Paso Mexi Pickles**

1 10-ounce can **Old El Paso Tomatoes and Green Chilies**
1 cup dairy sour cream
1/2 teaspoon salt
1/2 teaspoon ground coriander

. . .

1 3-ounce package cream cheese, softened
3/4 teaspoon salt
2 cups finely chopped cooked chicken
1/4 cup finely chopped green onion

. . .

Cooking oil
12 **Old El Paso Tortillas**
1 cup (4 ounces) shredded Monterey Jack or cheddar cheese

Reserve 1/4 cup of the tomatoes and green chilies. In blender container, combine remaining tomatoes and green chilies, the sour cream, the 1/2 teaspoon salt, and the coriander; cover and blend till smooth. Set aside.

Combine reserved tomatoes and green chilies, the cream cheese, and the 3/4 teaspoon salt; stir in chicken and onion.

In skillet, heat small amount of cooking oil. Dip tortillas, one at a time, into hot oil; fry just till limp, 5 seconds per side. Drain well. Spread cheese-chicken mixture on tortillas; roll up. Place, seam side down, in 12x7 1/2x2-inch baking dish. Cover with foil; bake in 350° oven for 30 minutes. In saucepan, heat sour cream mixture just till hot, do not boil. Pour over tortillas; sprinkle with cheese. Return to oven to melt cheese, 2 to 3 minutes. Makes 6 servings.

Turkey Enchiladas

For a zestier version try a 1/4 cup of **Old El Paso Jalapeño Relish** in the cheese sauce.

1 cup chopped onion
1 clove garlic, minced
2 tablespoons cooking oil
1 tablespoon all-purpose flour
1 16-ounce can tomatoes, cut up
1 15-ounce can tomato sauce
1 4-ounce can **Old El Paso Whole Green Chilies**, seeded, rinsed, and chopped
1 teaspoon sugar
1 teaspoon ground cumin
1/4 teaspoon salt

. . .

2 cups chopped cooked turkey
1 1/2 cups (6 ounces) shredded sharp American cheese
1/4 cup finely chopped onion
1/4 cup chopped pitted ripe olives
3/4 teaspoon salt

. . .

12 **Old El Paso Tortillas**
Cooking oil
1/4 cup sliced pitted ripe olives

Cook the 1 cup chopped onion and garlic in the 2 tablespoons cooking oil till onion is tender but not brown; stir in flour. Add undrained tomatoes, tomato sauce, chilies, sugar, cumin, and the 1/4 teaspoon salt. Cook and stir till thickened and bubbly; set aside.

Combine turkey, *half* the cheese, the 1/4 cup onion, the chopped olives, and the 3/4 teaspoon salt; set aside.

In skillet, dip tortillas in small amount of hot oil about 5 seconds per side or till tortillas are limp. Spoon 1/4 cup of the turkey mixture onto each tortilla; roll up.

Place filled tortillas in 13x9x2-inch baking dish. Pour tomato mixture over all. Bake, covered, in 350° oven for 15 minutes. Uncover; bake 15 minutes more or till heated through. Sprinkle with remaining shredded cheese; return to oven to melt cheese, 2 to 3 minutes more. Top with sliced olives. Makes 6 servings.

Zesty Western Enchiladas

Zesty Western Enchiladas

Pictured above

   3 tablespoons all-purpose flour
 ¹/₂ teaspoon salt
 ¹/₄ teaspoon paprika
 1¹/₂ cups milk
   1 10-ounce can **Old El Paso Hot Enchilada Sauce**
   1 cup (4 ounces) shredded cheddar cheese
 ¹/₂ cup sliced pitted ripe olives
 ³/₄ pound ground beef
 ¹/₂ cup chopped onion
   1 10¹/₂-ounce can **Old El Paso Jalapeño Bean Dip**
 ¹/₂ teaspoon salt
 ¹/₈ teaspoon pepper
  12 **Old El Paso Tortillas**
   1 large tomato, chopped

Microwave Cooking Directions: In 4-cup measure, combine flour, the ¹/₂ teaspoon salt, and the paprika. Stir in milk and enchilada sauce till blended. Micro-cook, uncovered, on high power, 2 minutes; stir. Micro-cook till bubbly, 4 to 5 minutes, stirring after each minute. Stir in cheese and olives till cheese melts; set sauce aside.

In glass bowl, crumble beef; add onion. Micro-cook, covered, on high power, about 5 minutes, stirring several times to break up meat. Drain off fat. Stir in bean dip, the remaining ¹/₂ teaspoon salt, and the pepper; mix well.

Wrap tortillas in paper toweling; micro-cook on high power 15 to 30 seconds or till warm.

On each tortilla, place about ¹/₃ cup meat mixture and 1 tablespoon tomato; roll up tightly. Place, seam side down, in 12x7¹/₂x2-inch baking dish. Pour cheese sauce over; micro-cook, uncovered, about 10 minutes, or till hot. Give dish half turns every 4 minutes. Makes 4 servings.

Mexican Meat Loaves

Cheesy Beef Pie
Pictured at right

1 pound ground beef
½ cup chopped onion
2 teaspoons cornstarch
1 10-ounce can **Old El Paso Mild Enchilada Sauce**
¼ cup snipped parsley
1 3-ounce can chopped mushrooms, drained

· · ·

2 packages (8 rolls each) refrigerated crescent rolls
3 eggs
6 slices (6 ounces) sharp process American cheese

In skillet, brown beef and onion; drain. Sprinkle meat with cornstarch; blend in. Stir in enchilada sauce, parsley, and mushrooms; set aside.

Unroll one package of rolls. Place the four sections of dough together, forming a 12x6-inch rectangle. Seal edges and perforations together. Roll to 12-inch square. Fit into 9-inch pie plate; trim edge even with plate. Separate one of the eggs; set yolk aside. Beat egg white with remaining two eggs; spread half over dough.

Spoon meat into shell. Arrange cheese slices atop; spread remaining egg mixture over cheese. Mix reserved yolk and 1 tablespoon water; brush lightly on edge of pastry. Reserve remaining yolk mixture. Roll second package of rolls to 12-inch square as before. Place atop filling. Trim about ½ inch beyond plate. Seal, and flute edge; cut slits for escape of steam. Brush top with remaining egg yolk mixture.

Bake in 350° oven for 50 to 55 minutes. If pastry gets too brown, cover with foil. Let stand 10 minutes before cutting. Makes 6 servings.

Chili Meat Loaf

2 slightly beaten eggs
1 8-ounce can tomatoes, cut up
½ of a 15-ounce can **Old El Paso Mexe-Beans,** drained
1 cup coarsely crushed **Old El Paso Taco** or **Tostada Shells**
¼ cup finely chopped green onion with tops
2 tablespoons snipped parsley
1½ teaspoons salt
1 teaspoon chili powder
2 pounds lean ground beef

· · ·

1 10-ounce can **Old El Paso Mild Enchilada Sauce**
½ cup (2 ounces) shredded sharp American cheese

Combine eggs, undrained tomatoes, beans, crushed taco shells, green onion, parsley, salt, and chili powder; mash beans slightly. Add ground beef; mix well. Shape into two 7x3x2-inch loaves. Tear off two 18-inch lengths of 18-inch wide heavy-duty foil. Place loaves on foil pieces; wrap foil around each loaf and seal securely. Grill over medium coals 30 minutes. Turn and grill 20 minutes more.

Meanwhile, in saucepan heat enchilada sauce. Open foil and fold down to make "pan." Continue cooking meat till done, about 10 minutes more, brushing frequently with enchilada sauce. Pass remaining sauce and cheese to top each serving. Makes 8 servings.

Crockery Cooker Directions: In bowl, combine eggs, 2 tablespoons of the enchilada sauce, undrained tomatoes, beans, crushed taco shells, green onion, parsley, salt, and chili powder. Add ground beef; mix well. Shape meat mixture into a round loaf slightly smaller in diameter than the crockery cooker. Place the meat loaf on rack in cooker so sides do not touch cooker.

Cover and cook on low-heat setting for 10 hours. In saucepan, heat the remaining enchilada sauce. Pass sauce and cheese to top each serving.

Cheesy Beef Pie

Meat and Potato Pie

Pictured on page 45

1 beaten egg
1/4 cup milk
1 envelope **Old El Paso Taco Seasoning Mix** (1/3 cup)
3/4 cup soft bread crumbs (1 slice bread)
1 pound ground beef
3 cups diced, cooked potatoes (3 medium potatoes)
1 4-ounce can **Old El Paso Taco Sauce**
1/4 cup chopped green onion
1 teaspoon prepared mustard
1/2 teaspoon salt
1/2 cup (2 ounces) shredded sharp American cheese

Combine egg, milk, taco seasoning mix, and bread crumbs; add beef and mix well. Press mixture into bottom and sides of 9-inch pie plate. Combine potatoes, taco sauce, onion, mustard, and salt; toss lightly. Spread in meat shell. Bake in 350° oven for 35 minutes. Remove from oven; sprinkle with cheese. Return to oven till cheese melts, about 3 minutes. Makes 6 servings.

Mexican Meat Loaf

1 slightly beaten egg
1/2 cup tomato sauce
1 4-ounce can **Old El Paso Whole Green Chilies**, seeded, rinsed, and chopped
1 3-ounce can chopped mushrooms, drained
1/3 cup fine dry bread crumbs
1 teaspoon salt
1 teaspoon chili powder
Dash pepper
1 1/2 pounds lean ground beef

. . .

3 slices (3 ounces) Monterey Jack cheese, quartered diagonally

Microwave Directions: In mixing bowl, combine egg, tomato sauce, chilies, mushrooms, crumbs, salt, chili powder, and pepper. Add meat; mix well. Invert a 2-inch diameter juice glass in center of an 8-inch round cake dish. Shape meat mixture in a ring around glass. Cover dish with waxed paper and micro-cook on high power about 14 minutes, turning dish a quarter-turn three times during cooking. Remove juice glass; drain off excess fat. Top meat with cheese; micro-cook, uncovered, 45 to 60 seconds more. Let stand 10 minutes before serving. Makes 6 servings.

Add interest to meat loaves—To win friends and influence your family, add new character to your next meat loaves with these ideas.
• Mix some **Old El Paso Chopped Green Chilies** into the meat mixture before shaping and baking.
• Use **Old El Paso Mild** or **Hot Enchilada Sauce** or **Taco Sauce** for the liquid in the meat loaf mixture.
• Pass **Old El Paso Taco Sauce** as a condiment or relish to top off meat loaf.
• Garnish the meat loaf platter with **Old El Paso Hot Pickled Yellow Chilies** or **Mexi Pickles**.
• Use an envelope of **Old El Paso Taco, Enchilada** or **Chili Seasoning Mix** to season the meat mixture.
• The last few minutes of baking, layer strips of **Old El Paso Whole Green Chilies** and cheese alternately atop of the meat loaf.

INDEX